The Economics of the Law

The Economics of the Law

Frank H. Stephen
Reader in Economics
University of Strathclyde

Iowa State University Press/Ames

Frank H. Stephen is Reader in Economics
at the University of Strathclyde

© 1988 Frank H. Stephen

Published in the United States and Canada
by the Iowa State University Press, Ames, Iowa 50010

Published simultaneously in Great Britain by
Wheatsheaf Books Ltd, Brighton, Sussex BN1 1AD

Printed in England

First edition, 1988

Library of Congress Cataloging-in-Publication Data
Stephen, Frank H., 1946–
    The economics of the law.

    Includes bibliographical references and index.
    1. Law — United States.   2. Economics.   I. Title.
KF380.S73   1988   349.73   88-8872
ISBN 0-8138-0194-X   347.3

To Christine, Kate and Lucy

Contents

Preface

The writing of this book would not have taken place without the support and encouragement of a number of people. Most important are the contributors to the growing law-and-economics literature without whom there would be little to write. My interest in the use of economic reasoning in the area of the law was nurtured during many commuting journeys with Eric Young.

I could not have immersed myself so freely in this literature without the benefit of a sabbatical term spend at the Faculty of Law at the University of Toronto. This was made possible by the generosity of the University of Strathclyde in granting me leave, the British Academy for its financial support, and the Connaught Fund grant to the Faculty of Law in Toronto. I also benefited from visits to Yale, Chicago and Northwestern Universities and the Law Institute for Economics Professors held at Dartmouth College, New Hampshire under the auspices of Henry Manne. During this period I benefited from discussions with a number of people including Guido Calabresi, Bob Ellickson, Richard Epstein, Victor Goldberg, Henry Hansmann, Bill Landes, Anthony Ogus, George Priest, Rob Prichard, Steven Shavell, Michael Trebilcock, Oliver Williamson and Arnie Weinberg. I am grateful to the Carnegie Fund for the Universities of Scotland whose financial assistance made these visits possible.

I am also most grateful to the members of the Law School at the University of Strathclyde who have answered my many questions concerning law. Particular thanks are due to Eric Young who not only encouraged my interest in the subject but read the first draft of this material in its entirety. Anthony Ogus was kind enough to read all of the text. Any remaining errors are decidedly my own.

The typescript was prepared with skill and great fortitude by Irene Nugent and Morag Pryce. I am most grateful to my wife Christine and my daughters Kate and Lucy who have put up with much in the book's preparation and to whom it is dedicated.

1 Introduction

In the last two decades or so the academic study of law, particularly in North America, has witnessed an increased use of economic concepts and modes of reasoning. This book is an attempt to synthesise this growing literature in a way which makes it accessible to students and academics in both disciplines without overselling the significance of the economic approach to the law. The reader should be clear from the outset what this book is *not* about. It is not about the traditional interactions of the two subjects, e.g. anti-trust or competition law: these are concerned with the regulation, by statute or courts, of economic behaviour. Nor is it about the economic evaluation of particular items of, legislation: cost-benefit analysis or impact analysis. It is about the application of economic modes of analysis to legal rules and doctrines. Given the assumptions about human behaviour and motivation commonly made by economists, what are the implications for legal rules and doctrines? What are the implications of economic concepts such as 'efficiency' for the design of legal rules. The literature which embodies these concerns has come to be designated 'law-and-economics' to distinguish it from other areas of intersection of the two disciplines. Viewed by the legal scholar, this book is a somewhat narrow approach to jurisprudence. Viewed by the economist, it is the application of the tools of his trade to a specific area of social activity.

Law-and-economics is now an integral part of legal education in many of the most distinguished law schools in North America, both as a course in its own right and as a component of courses in torts, contracts and property. It has been argued that it is no longer possible to be a 'serious theorist in tort law or contract law without at least being familiar with, and taking account of, the economic analysis in these fields' (Hansmann, 1983). The subject however, has not had the same impact on the eastern shores of the Atlantic.

What economics is providing here is a theoretical framework for analysing the law: a means of deriving predictions about behaviour given 'the law' or a means of deriving a set of rules to produce desired behaviour. This is a very different approach from that of traditional legal scholarship. Much of that scholarship is devoted to interpreting cases. It is an *inductive* process in which the cases are examined to see what categories emerge. In contrast, the economic approach is *deductive*. Assumptions are made about human behaviour and the implications of these for specific circumstances are deduced. This 'model-building' approach may perceive (or indeed seek out) categories implicit in the cases. As later chapters of this book will demonstrate, whilst legal doctrine treats nuisance, torts and contract as separate compartments, law-and-economics focuses on very definite similarities among the problems dealt with in these doctrines.

The terms normative, positive and descriptive law-and-economics have been imported from economic methodology to categorise different applications of economics to the law (see Burrows and Veljanovski, 1981; Veljanovski, 1982). Normative theories are those which embody value-judgements and imply an exhortation, e.g. 'The government *should* ensure all markets are competitive'. This statement embodies the value-judgement that competition is a desirable objective of public policy. As such it is not a matter of fact but a belief. On the other hand, a positive statement is a question of fact and can therefore, in principle, be subjected to scientific test, e.g. 'the sun will rise tomorrow' is a refutable or testable hypothesis. Provided observers agree on the meaning of the words used, we only have to observe what happens tomorrow to test the hypothesis. Descriptive economics, according to Veljanovski (1982), attempts to model actual processes and to describe the economic influences that affect them. The normative/positive distinction has come in for increasing criticism as economists have become more sophisticated in their appreciation of methodology.

Much of what is described as positive economics in textbooks is really *prescriptive* (Machlup, 1969). It prescribes the behaviour (or rules) necessary to obtain a stated goal without necessarily suggesting that the goal should be an object of public policy. Consider the statement that to maximise profits firms should equate marginal revenue and marginal cost. This neither says that firms actually equate marginal revenue and marginal cost (therefore it is not positive) nor that firms ought to equate them, nor that they ought to maximise profits (thus it is not normative). The statement is prescriptive: if profit-maximisation is desired, marginal revenue and marginal cost must be equated. The proposition may also be described as analytical (see McLachlan and Swales, 1982). Most of the law-and-economics in this book is analytical/prescriptive in this sense in that it analyses the efficiency implications of different legal doctrines without arguing that efficiency should be the touchstone of legal doctrines. In the final chapter of this book some normative propositions will be addressed.

The term positive law-and-economics is usually used to describe two somewhat different approaches: one concerned with *prediction* and one with *description*. A number of economists following the lead given by Milton Friedman take the view that one of the roles of economic theory is to allow us to predict human behaviour. Consequently the validity of a theory is to be judged by the correspondence of its predictions to the 'facts'. Thus, whether or not a theory's assumptions are realistic or descriptively accurate is irrelevant so long as the theory is predictively accurate. Although for a number of years this approach was labelled 'positivist', in recent years academics concerned with economic methodology have come to recognise that it is more correctly described as 'instrumentalist' (see Caldwell, 1983).

The predictive (or instrumentalist) approach has been used very successfully in one area of intersection between law and economics: the economics of crime. Here models of individual and household behaviour have been used to develop predictions about the response of criminals or potential criminals to different detection and sentencing policies (Becker and Landes, 1974; Heineke, 1978; Wolpin, 1978). This, however, is not law-and-economics as we have defined it. It is really straightforward economics and has had little impact on legal scholars. We therefore, do not discuss that literature in this book.

The second sub-category associated with the term positive law-and-economics is what Burrows and Veljanovski (1982) call descriptive law and economics. This has had a greater impact on legal scholars. Here 'the structure of the legal system itself' is the focus of analysis. As these authors point out, the weakness of assumptions is much more important here because such theories require to have substantive descriptive content and the assumptions themselves require to be verifiable. (For a discussion of the role of assumptions and the relevance of their realism, see Caldwell, 1983.)

The early thrust of 'descriptive' law-and-economics arose from the work of R.A. Posner, Professor of Law in the Chicago Law School. (At the time of writing Professor Posner is a Justice of the US 7th Circuit Court of Appeals.) Starting in Posner (1972b), he argued that the implicit goal of the common law was the promotion of an efficient allocation of resources. The doctrines, remedies and procedures of the common law are seen to be consistent with the pursuit of efficiency. This work stimulated both emulation and criticism: whole issues of North American law journals were devoted to its discussion. The problems associated with evaluating this claim are discussed in the final chapter of this book. For the moment it is sufficient to say that the claim is more sceptically received now than it once was. A more modest formulation of Posner's descriptive claim has been suggested by Professor Frank Michelman of Harvard Law School: 'that the rules, taken as a whole, tend to look as though they were chosen, with a view to maximizing social wealth (economic output as measures by price) by judges subscribing to a certain set of ('micro-economic') theoretical principles' (Michelman, 1979).

This formulation suggests that judges do not consciously maximise social wealth but that they behave *as if* they did. This is more in line with the instrumentalist approach rather than the descriptive approach. For an example of an empirical study in the spirit of Michelman's statement, see Stephen and Young (1985). The descriptive claim amounts, in effect, to saying that a set of legal rules or judicial decisions can be rationalised (i.e. made consistent) by imputing an economic (or economist's) rationale to it. This does, of course, raise the common problem of inductive reasoning: that there may be many rationales consistent with a given set of events or 'facts'.

The use of economics to provide the rationale underlying legal rules and judicial decisions has been suggested in a slightly different way by another legal scholar. L.A. Kornhauser (1980) suggests that economics might be seen as a source of 'behavioural hypotheses' or 'insights' in to the study of the law. Indeed, much of the scholarship discussed in this book can be seen in this light: models of human behaviour commonly adopted in economics are used to try to provide a better understanding of the law and its consequences.

What Michelman and Kornhauser (and many others) are pointing to is the differences between the methodology of the traditional legal scholar and the traditional economics scholar. It is the latter which provides the methodology of law-and-economics. Much traditional legal scholarship is devoted to interpreting cases: an inductive approach in which cases are examined to see what categories emerge. The economist's approach, on the other hand, is deductive: assumptions and the implications of these assumptions for behaviour under specific conditions or circumstances are deduced. This approach has (somewhat grandiosely) come to be described as 'model-building'. It is an approach which may perceive (or indeed seek out) categories implicit in the cases. What it provides is a free-standing framework for analysis which is independent of the particular materials being investigated: a general theory. (For more on these points, see Coase, 1977; Klevorick, 1983.)

The preceding discussion may give the impression that legal scholarship has a great deal to gain from economics whilst there is little to be gained by economists from legal scholarship. This is not so. Yet there is a danger that law-and-economics may be seen as a colonisation of legal scholarship by economists: a part of a wider imperialism through which economics has expanded its boundaries into terrain previously inhabited by other social science disciplines. Ronald Coase

(1977) has argued that such a movement cannot be based solely on techniques since the techniques of economics will be quickly learned by the other social scientists who will have the advantage of being more familiar with, and sensitive to, the terrain in which the techniques are to be applied. To some extent what has happened in law-and-economics bears this out. Many legal scholars have been quick to absorb the techniques and method of economics which they are able to use to great effect in the area of law in which they have a comparative advantage over economists. However, some of the early work in this field exhibited the over-enthusiasm and lack of subtlety of both the recent convert and the campaigning missionary.

But Coase (1977) made another point: economics has much to gain from forays into foreign terrain because they will make economists aware of the effect that other dimensions of the social system have on the functioning of the economic system. In particular, economists who have worked beyond the traditional boundaries of their subject have to become particularly aware of the important effect that social institutions have on human behaviour. The law is an important and pervasive social institution. An area where economics has benefited from contact with other social sciences is what has come to be known as 'transaction cost economics'. This will be discussed more fully in the latter part of Chapter 8 when we discuss contract. The point of direct relevance here is that law-and-economics is a two-way street: both economists and lawyers can learn a great deal to the benefit of their own scholarship from it. However, both must be sensitive to its limitations. As Michael Trebilcock (1983) has pointed out, the more sophisticated law-and-economics has become the less-clear-cut are its implications for policy.

This book is divided into two parts. Part I deals with economic concepts, whilst Part II analyses legal doctrines and institutions using these economic concepts. This division allows readers familiar with the economic concepts to go straight to their application. All economists will be familiar with the material of Chapter 4. Fewer will, I think, be familiar with Chapters 2 and 3. Whilst the Coase Theorem has had sufficient impact on the mainstream economics literature to be discussed in intermediate microeconomics textbooks (e.g. Call and Holahan, 1980), as well as the literature on externalities, non-specialists are unlikely to be familiar with all of the subtleties and limitations discussed in Chapter 3. Similarly, general ideas about property rights have permeated the mainstream literature without everyone becoming familiar with the literature discussed in Chapter 2. Non-economists should not find the pace at which the concepts are introduced too quick. In teaching lawyers I have found that absorption of the economic concepts is aided by introducing them in the context of a legal discussion. Consequently, I weave the material of Chapters 2 and 3 into the material of Chapter 5. However, this approach is not so readily transferred to the printed medium. In addition it would make for tedious reading by those competent in economics. If the book is being used as the basis of a course for non-economists I would suggest that the interweaving be undertaken.

Part II does not represent a comprehensive treatment of legal doctrines using economic concepts. Neither space nor competence permits this. Such an approach is provided in Posner (1977). The focus here is on property, tort and contract. However the treatment of these topics is far from exhaustive. Each of them could give rise to a sizeable book, as indeed they have (e.g. Ackerman, 1975; Posner, 1982; and Kronman and Posner, 1979). The approach here is to introduce the subject and give an insight of its usefulness and limitations. Chapter 6 has three main sections dealing with conflicts in the use of property (nuisance), the compulsory acquisition of private property by the State (eminent domain and compulsory purchase), and the public regulation of land use (zoning and development control). Thus both common law and public law doctrines in respect of property are examined using economic concepts introduced in Part I, together with the property rules/liability rules framework discussed in Chapter 5. Chapter 7 turns to tort (or delict as it is called in Scotland), a second pillar of the common law. Here the doctrines of strict liability, negligence, contributory negligence and comparative negligence are examined both in terms of efficiency and from the perspective of distributive justice. The economics of contract law is the subject-matter of Chapter 8.

Here such topics as consumer warranties, standard-form contracts and damage for contract breach are analysed. The transactions cost or neo-institutional approach to contract is introduced here. In the final chapter the claim that the common law is efficient is examined, as well as Posner's claim that value-maximisation is the only ethically justified basis for the common law. The final part of the chapter (and the book) outlines Paul Rubin's evolutionary theory of the common law.

Part I
Economic Concepts

2 Property rights

INTRODUCTION

Much economic analysis is conducted in the abstract with little concern for the details of institutional arrangements such as what obligations attend the payment of a sum of money to purchase a good. Economists just talk vaguely about exchanges. However, over the last thirty years or so a number of economists have become concerned with what they have called *property rights*. Essentially these boil down to the rights of an individual, but the economist's notion of property is much broader than that of the lawyer. It includes both tort and contract law, common and statutory law, civil and criminal law, vested and non-vested rights and civil rights. It includes informal practices and traditions embedded in culture as well as formal legal institutions.

To the economist property rights are not relationships between men and things but, as Furubotn and Pejovich (1972) express it: 'the sanctioned behavioural relations among men that arise from the existence of things and pertain to their use'. Property rights specify norms of behaviour with respect to 'things' that everyone must observe in interactions with others or *bear the penalty for non-observance*. The prevailing system of property rights are therefore the set of economic and social relations defining the position of each individual with respect to the utilisation of scarce resources.

That resources are scarce in our world is a datum of economic analysis. Human wants are unlimited but the resources (natural or man-made) to satisfy them are finite. In

11

the absence of well-defined property rights, the use to which resources would be put would be determined on a first-come first-served basis (or actually on a might is right basis) without property rights and a means to enforce them, the use to which a resource is put would be almost capricious. As soon as one person starts to cultivate a plot of land to grow vegetables someone else might let his cattle roam on the field eating and destroying the crop; someone else might slaughter the cattle to obtain food, etc.

Notice that the wide definition of property rights we have used does not require that resources be specifically allocated to individuals as *private* property (although, as will be seen below, many economists come to that conclusion because of assumptions which they make about motivation). The system of behavioural relationships in a society might be such that all 'property' is communally held, and a system of custom and convention dictates who will do which tasks and how the products of those tasks will be allocated amongst the members of that society. Such a system would, of course, require sanctions to be imposed upon those who break with custom or tradition and would probably involve some means of social education which inculcated the members of the society with the appropriate norms and mores. There would still be property rights: the relationship of one person to another *vis-à-vis* a physical entity would have to be defined (if only implicitly by tradition).

PRIVATE PROPERTY AND EFFICIENCY

Much of the property rights literature in economics tends to the view that well-defined *private* property rights are superior to communal or public property rights. 'Superiority' is of course in this context defined in terms of *efficiency*. (A situation is said to be efficient if it is not possible to so reallocate resources such that someone can be made better off without making someone else worse off.) Essentially it is argued that an absence of well-defined private property rights reduces incentives for individuals to make the best use of resources to which they have access.

Note, here, that this argument hinges on the motivations of the individual. Economists *assume* that individuals are motivated to maximise utility (satisfaction or well-being), i.e. they generally assume them to be motivated by self-interest. Thus if an individual does not *own* a plot of land (in the sense of having a legal interest in it) he is assumed not to be concerned with keeping it productive beyond the period during which he will use it. Thus he will not apply appropriate nutrient to it nor use appropriate crop rotations but get what he can from it and put as little into it as possible. Economists believe this to be so because the individual has no reasonably assured reward for incurring such costs. The situation would be different if there were some mechanism by which the individual could be compensated for these expenditures – perhaps by proof that he had undertaken them. This would give him some form of property right.

However, if the individual were merely compensated for the costs incurred he would have only a limited incentive to make the effort. If he were to make some profit, i.e. earn a return comparable to that which he could from expending the same resources (of time and money) in its next best use, he might have some incentive to do so. Thus, it is argued, the way to ensure the efficient use of the land (or other property) is to give someone a perpetual interest in it which can be sold; i.e. it should be *transferable*.

The transferability of the property right is thought to provide the farmer, for example, with an incentive to use and maintain land efficiently. Given current and prospective prices for different products of the land and the costs of other resources used to produce them, the farmer will use the land in the most profitable way and land will be shifted from low-valued uses to high-valued ones. The farmer will not only have an incentive to make good current use but he will also have an incentive to maintain the productivity of the land asset. He will be encouraged to undertake investment expenditures which if he had a short (and uncertain) right to the land would not be worthwhile, e.g. applying fertilisers, laying drains, planting hedges, etc. In effect, he is encouraged to behave as if he were going to utilise the land in perpetuity because at any time he (or his heirs when he dies) can capitalise the future profits from these expenditures by selling the right in the land to someone else.

Transferability is a *necessary* condition for attaining efficiency but it is not a *sufficient* condition: it does not guarantee efficiency. First, transfer must be relatively easy. If the transaction costs are high relative to the value of the asset, transferability in *principle* may not be worth much in *practice*. Secondly, transferability would not be worth much if there were not also a right of *exclusivity*. The property right must guarantee the exclusive use of the land otherwise someone else might be able to gain the benefits of using the land without making the expenditures.

As a first step we might simply say that a right of complete exclusion would help to produce efficiency: anyone who wants to use the land in any way would have to purchase that right from the farmer. This would apply to ramblers, governments or anyone else. We shall later see why it might be in the interests of efficiency to qualify this right.

So far the discussion has focused on the efficient use of a *single* piece of land. In order that resources be allocated efficiently it has been argued that someone must have exclusive and transferable rights in it. To complete the property rights theorist's prescription, all we need to add is that if this applies to one piece of land it applies to all pieces of land (and by extension to all forms of property). Thus a third condition is that of *universality*.

In summary, there are three necessary conditions for the attainment of efficiency relating to property rights:

(i) *Universality*: all scarce resources should be owned by someone.
(ii) *Exclusivity*: property rights should be exclusive rights.
(iii) *Transferability*: this is necessary to ensure that resources will be transferred from low-valued uses to high-valued uses.

The three taken together ensure that some individual has the incentive to ensure that all resources are used efficiently, i.e. in their highest valued use, because that is where the individual receives the greatest reward.

In reality, it is not possible to meet the property rights

theorists' prescription in full. In particular, it is not possible to allocate property rights universally: some resources by their very nature are communal. To understand this, consider air pollution. Atmosphere is a resource which is being used to absorb waste materials from production: e.g. smoke. We cannot allocate property rights over the air to individuals: for one thing, they move about too much! Thus no one can *own* it and anyone can use it, consequently no one has incentive to use it efficiently. The cost of polluting the atmosphere does not fall on the pollutor; it's a free good to him and, therefore, in deciding his level of production he does not count it as a cost. Consequently, he will use too much of it. Everyone is in the same position, thus everyone uses too much. In many jurisdictions the state has effectively asserted property rights over the air by enacting legislation to control atmospheric pollution (i.e. the use to which that atmosphere may be put). Paradoxically, the power of the property rights argument is perhaps best illustrated when the three conditions cannot be fulfilled.

TESTING THE THEORY

Much has been written in recent years by economists on the importance of property rights for efficiency. Much of this literature is theoretical, arguing from assumptions about human motivation to prescriptions for economic policy. What evidence is there for the theory?

Casual empiricism is frequently used to support the argument that private property rights generate efficiency: we can all cite examples of the private abuse of common property such as vandalism, pollution, etc. Broad historical generalisation also seems to support this view: the association of economic growth with the spread of private property and capitalism. These, however, do not fit the bill for the type of evidence that most scientists would require to test a theory. What is needed is evidence that at least in principle allows the possibility of refuting the hypothesis under test. It has to be admitted that whilst most economists profess adherence to this 'scientific method' much of the evidence adduced in support of economic theories fails to satisfy this rigorous prescription.

Ideally, having introduced the economist's view of property rights we should test the predictions (or hypotheses) for behaviour against the evidence of actual behaviour. One area where such evidence should be available is the fishing industry. This is usually the classic example quoted of a non-owned resource subject to inefficiency: fish stocks are not owned by anyone therefore no one has an incentive to husband them efficiently, to provide for a long-term maintenance of stocks, etc. However, rigorous tests of the benefits of exclusivity are not easy to come by. Much has been written on this topic but much of it is theoretical prediction or implicit theorising (interpreting facts in the light of one theory rather than testing the theory against the facts).

To be fair, subjecting hypotheses such as those relating to property rights to refutation does present substantial problems: ideally one requires situations where, for example, common property rights and private property rights coexist with all other factors held constant (i.e. a true experimental situation). This is not commonly available. Often what is available is evidence on economic performance as property rights have changed over time. However, it is unlikely that nothing other than property rights have changed. Can we make adequate allowance for all the other things that have changed? Alternatively we might have evidence on contemporaneous differences in property rights. But again, are all other things the same? Can we control for other changes?

This is the classic economic problem of the *ceteris paribus* (other things equal) assumption in economics: very seldom are they *cetera paria*. Luckily, multivariate statistical techniques can help us here but that requires good data which are not always available.

Exclusivity

With these caveats in mind let us look at some of the evidence. De Alessi (1980) reports a study of land tenure in Libya carried out by Bottomley and reported in *Land Economics* in 1963. The study focuses on the Libyan province of Tripolitania where 97 per cent of land is held in common. It is suggested that 'at least some of this land was physically as fertile as much of the land held privately'. What do property rights theorists predict will happen in such circumstances? Because of the absence of exclusivity and transferability there is no incentive to invest in the common land. By investment an economist means undertaking outlays now in the expectation of reaping benefits in the future. In the present context this means an absence of investment in irrigation or other measures to increase the fertility of the land. Nor would we expect to find the planting of crops with long gestation periods. We would also expect that the investment would be in privately owned 'capital'.

Bottomley's evidence suggests that the common land was subject to occasional planting of crops of barley wherever rain seemed adequate, and to over-grazing by privately owned sheep and goats. There was less investment in irrigation on common land as compared to privately owned land. Consequently the maximum returns per hectare were much lower for commonly owned land than privately owned land.

Given the relative absence of privately owned land it is to be expected that it would fetch very high rents and consequently be more intensively cultivated. This is likely to lead to high capital-to-labour ratios in cultivation. As more and more capital is used this is likely to mean that the additional output gained from each additional unit of capital employed will fall (diminishing returns). In contrast, on commonly owned land little capital is used and, therefore, it would be expected that the marginal product of capital will be higher on common land than on private land. Conversely, the marginal product of labour is expected to be higher on private land than on common land. Bottomley found exactly this.

Similar sorts of evidence have been found in the US coastal oyster industry in a study by Agnello and Donnelley (1975). A number of US coastal states have identified what are considered natural oyster beds and defined them as a common property resource. Other areas, however, are available on private leases. Property rights theory would predict that the commonly owned oyster grounds would be cultivated more labour-intensely and therefore have lower labour productivity than the privately owned grounds. Using data for 16 Atlantic and Gulf Coast states average labour productivity (weight of meat/labour force) was calculated and regression analysis used to show the effects of ownership form, amount of capital, opportunity wage of labour, and the incidence of MSX disease. Labour productivity was higher on privately owned oyster grounds when account was taken of these other factors. Agnello and Donnelley also looked at data over a longer period for Virginia and Maryland which are contiguous and economically similar. This might be thought to control for other omitted variables. The results again supported the view that labour productivity was positively associated with private ownership.

Another implication of the property rights argument is that under common ownership there is an incentive to harvest early for fear that if you do not someone else will. Agnello and Donnelley (1975) found that for Virginia and Maryland for the period 1965–70 the quantity of oysters harvested earlier in the season was larger for commonly owned beds than for private beds. It is also argued that earlier harvesting implies lower prices and this was found for all 16 states in the main study. Lower average state price was found to be related to a higher proportion of commonly owned oyster beds. Revenue per worker was similarly related to ownership characteristics.

Further evidence on the effects of common property rights can be obtained by looking at what happens when there is a complete absence of property rights. The classic case is fishing. Most readers will be aware of the problem of over-fishing. Sea fish stocks are not owned by anyone, therefore no one has an incentive to husband them, but everyone has an incentive to harvest them. The outcome of this is the likelihood that (in the absence of some form of state control) over-fishing will take place, i.e. more fish will be caught than is desirable to sustain the stocks.

There is a commonly held belief in the need to regulate catches in order to ensure the long-run survival of species. This perceived need might itself be taken as evidence of what happens when a resource is not owned and indeed cannot effectively be owned. We can, however, go further and report one study of this phenomenon (though related to lobster fisheries) published in 1972 by F. W. Bell. Bell demonstrates that the number of lobster traps actually in use in the inshore lobster fisheries of Northern US and Canada were close to those that maximised the profits of individual fishermen, given the price at which lobster meat sold. That is, he found that price approximated long-run average cost. However, there were twice the number of traps economically desirable from the social point of view (i.e. the number of traps which would yield catch where price would be equal to long-run *marginal* cost). Thus for much of the lobster meat yield the cost of capturing an additional pound exceeded the price at which it sold.

The phenomenon arises because when the number of traps gets beyond a certain point the weight of lobster caught starts to fall (i.e. over-fishing). The private incentive of the individual fishermen is not in harmony with social interest. It should be noted that Bell's concept of the social interest is an economic one and does not relate to the optimum physical size of the stock of fish.

Another area where common pool problems arise is in on-shore oilfields in the USA. Interestingly, however, the problem arises not because of the absence of private property rights but because of their presence.

The discussion which follows is based on research reported by Gary Libecap and Steven Wiggins (Wiggins and Libecap, 1985; Libecap and Wiggins, 1985). Libecap and Wiggins are actually concerned with explaining why private bargaining does not generate the unitisation of US on-shore oilfields. What is of interest in the present context is the benefit to be gained from unitisation.

In the United States mineral rights are held by surface landowners. Landownership is typically widely dispersed. The extent of the reservoir of oil under the surface will be determined by geological factors unrelated to the pattern of surface landownership. Oil is migratory and when it is extracted from one part of the field, oil from other parts of the field flows towards the areas from which it has been extracted. The ownership of the oil cannot, therefore, be determined until it has been extracted from the reservoir. The consequence of this is that the reservoir of oil is actually a common property resource for everyone who has the right to drill on the surface land. These people have an incentive to extract the oil quickly before someone else does. However, a large number of wells operating in competition reduces surface pressure, the natural gas dissolved in the oil comes out of solution, reducing the oil's mobility and leaving some reserves permanently trapped below ground. This raises the cost of extraction. The technical solution to this is to handle the reservoir as a unit combining extraction and pumping of oil or gas to maintain pressure. In a non-unitised field there is no incentive to maintain pressure as it will benefit others. The competitive extraction of the oil dissipates the profits of the field. As Libecap and Wiggins have demonstrated, the differences in yield from unitised and non-unitised fields can be enormous.

The evidence presented on the preceding pages supports the arguments of the earlier part of this chapter that an absence of exclusive property rights leads to an inefficient utilisation of resources. However, it cannot be taken as necessarily supporting exclusive *private* property rights. The oilfield unitisation example shows that state intervention to limit the exercise of the landowner's property rights can increase efficiency by giving an exclusive right to extract oil (but not the income from it) to a designated operator. Similar benefits are obtained in jurisdictions where mineral rights are vested in the state rather than the surface landowner and the licence to extract the mineral over geographically meaningful areas is auctioned by the state. Presumably similar regulatory intervention would be possible, in principle, in the case of fisheries. This would differ from the most common forms of fisheries regulation which are based on catch size, boat size and net size.

Transferability
The most direct implication of the condition of transferability, from the economist's point of view, is in transferability of use: the ease with which property can be transferred from a low valued use to a high valued use. In so far as the price system reflects the value of resources to society, any blockage to the smooth transfer of a resource from one use to another impairs 'social efficiency'. This explains the hostility of many economists to regulation and, in particular, land-use regulation which stops land being allocated to its most highly

valued use. As we shall see in a later chapter, there are occasions when such regulation or attenuation of property rights is efficient.

An absence of transferability will hamper investment in some circumstances. Take for example where there is only a *usufruct* (right of use) with a limited time horizon such as that enjoyed by a tenant with no or an imperfect right of recovering investments in land, or that of a member of a producer's cooperative who has a right only to share in its income while he works in the cooperative. Consider the latter of these: members share in the proceeds of a cooperative's effort only as long as they work in it. In the most common traditional form of cooperative the right to that income ceases on retirement or on transfer to another firm.

What attitude will the member of such a cooperative have to the purchase of new plant or equipment? If this purchase is to be financed from within the firm from retained earnings this implies that each member's dividend from current operations is reduced. The return to this investment is that the productivity of the firm in the future will be higher because of this new plant and equipment. Typically, however, that return will only accrue over a number of years and members of the cooperative nearing retirement or likely to move to another firm may feel unwilling to give up income now for the prospect of a return which they will not be around to benefit from. This has led many economists to argue that such cooperatives are doomed to failure because they will be short-sighted with respect to investment. What is needed is some mechanism whereby cooperative members can capture some of the as yet unearned return from their investment when they leave, i.e. their share should not only be transferable but marketable. Evidence which has been assembled seems to suggest that the economically successful cooperatives such as those of Mondragon in Spain and the US Pacific coast plywood industry are those that provide some form of transferability of property right (see further Stephen, 1984).

Evolution of Property Rights
The discussion so far has looked at property rights in a very static way: how the existing system of property rights affect

things. Property rights theorists would argue that property rights will themselves change over time as relative values and incentives change. This approach treats the evolution of property rights as a single aspect of a wider theory of institutional change. Leading exponents of this view are the American economic historians Lance Davis and Douglass North in their *Institutional Change and American Economic Growth*: 'It is the possibility of profits that cannot be captured within the existing arrangemental structure that leads to the formation of new (or mutations of old) institutional arrangements.' In this view new property rights may be created in response to changing economic pressures or opportunities. As population pressures grow resources that were previously treated as common property may become assigned as private property in order to allocate them to the most efficient use. As technology changes, resources which were incapable of private assignment (or policing) at low cost become so. This will make it possible for private property rights to be exercised. An often quoted example of this is the advent of barbed wire and its introduction in the western United States. As profitable uses for previously unappropriated land are found rules governing appropriation will develop.

As an example of the last of these consider the development of mineral rights in the western United States. Gary Libecap (1978; 1979) has studied the evolution of mineral rights in relation to the development of the Comstock Load in Nevada. The thesis here is that mineral rights law in the American West did not evolve autonomously but in response to economic forces. Originally the Comstock mines were on federally owned land. In 1858 there was no means by which private ownership could be granted yet there were about 100 miners in the Comstock area operating in an area of 40 square miles under unwritten and informal agreements. Total annual production was valued at less than $67,000. It is asserted that the land was not valuable enough for a more formal (and costly) definition of property rights.

The Comstock Load was discovered in January 1859. It was a rich vein of ore bearing quartz with a mineralised zone about five miles long and one mile wide. Output rose to $260,000 by the end of 1859 and was running at an annual rate of $2.5

million by 1861, by which time the population of the area was 20,000. Between 1859 and 1861 3149 claims had been made to portions of the Comstock Load or adjacent veins. This led to the formation of formal mining camp governments at Gold Hill, Virginia City and Devil's Gate. These had written rules regarding the establishment and maintenance of private holdings, a permanent claims recorder and *ad hoc* miners' courts. The rules described the recording requirements for locating a claim, the size of individual allotments, the procedures for marking claim boundaries, and the work requirement necessary to maintain ownership. *These rules followed on competition for land, they did not precede it.* The rise in output continued, signalling an increased value of rights and the workload quickly swamped the miners' courts. The conflicts were centred mostly on the Comstock Load.

Between 1860 and 1865 the mines became more capital-intensive as the exhaustion of surface deposits necessitated the sinking of deep shafts (57 miles) and associated processing plants. This necessitated a change in ownership with the corporate form predominating. These were largely floated on the San Francisco stock exchange. Both the scale and the absentee ownership of the mines led to pressure for a more formal judicial authority: the drive for territorial status. This meant that decisions of the courts would be recognised outside the area (i.e. in California). Part of the cost would also be borne by Congress. In March 1861 the Nevada Territorial Government was created and the legislature set about creating a judicial system, predominantly to deal with mineral rights.

By 1861 most of the disputes in the court involved the most productive mines on the Comstock Load and parallel and competing claims. The mining camp rules were clear on defining boundaries between claims on the same vein of rock but not on boundaries between mines on different veins. This was related to extra-lateral rights which allowed claims to follow their section of the vein wherever it travelled underground. Thus one claim could run under another so long as they were on separate veins. The owners of rich Comstock mines were vigorous on defending their claims: 70 per cent of cases involved them as plaintiffs mostly in actions of ejectment.

The territorial government provided for only three judges

who by 1864 were overwhelmed by the caseload. There was a massive backlog which became part of the pressure for statehood which would provide for a more extensive judicial system. Further pressure for statehood came from the Federal government's need to raise revenue for its Civil War debt. The selling or taxing of western mineral lands might be a source of this. This would override the essentially local rights structure which was not formally recognised by Congress. Statehood was a way of blocking this and it came in October 1864.

By 1865 judicial rulings had settled the basis of sub-surface boundaries and litigation eased off. Indeed after 1866 the state legisture ceased meeting annually and began to meet biennially. Between 1863 and 1868 the Nevada Supreme Court had 32 mineral rights cases, but between 1869 and 1875 there were only seven. Gary Libecap has constructed an index of legal change in Nevada based on legislation and court rulings covering fifteen headings of importance in mining law. All legislation and verdicts were screened to see whether they involved change in any of these areas: in particular, were they more detailed and precise in their definition of rights? This was used to calculate an index of increase in specifity of mineral rights. Cumulative indices for statutes and for court rulings were constructed. The value of this was seen to increase rapidly between 1859 and 1868, rise more slowly to the 1880s and are largely constant thereafter, as illustrated in Figure 2.1

The data were analysed statistically. The annual change in the precision of the law was related to average output of the Comstock Load and the total precision of the law. For the period 1858–1868 output was the most significant determinant of the change in precision (total precision had a negative but statistically insignificant effect). From 1869–75 output had a smaller and statistically insignificant effect, whilst total precision was insignificant. In the period 1859–95 output had a negative but statistically insignificant effect, whilst that of total precision had a negative and statistically significant effect. These results are consistent with the view that Nevada mining law was determined by the value of the mineral rights to the Comstock Load.

A test was also carried out relating the annual change in the precision of the law to the gap between the final precision and

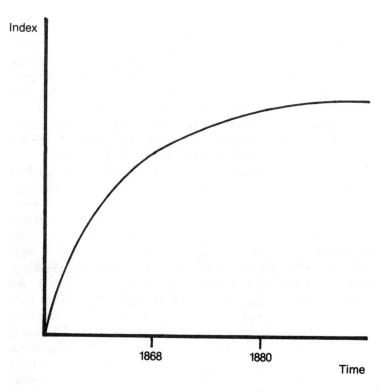

Figure 2.1

current precision. This was found to be highly significant, and explained 82 per cent of variation in the annual charge, i.e. the data are consistent with the view that the law evolved as the result of an adjustment process to reduce ownership uncertainty. This study by Libecap makes a persuasive case study of how economic factors can shape the evolution of property rights.

SUMMARY

This chapter has introduced the modern economic concept of property rights. Although it has been argued that efficiency will be enhanced by universality, exclusivity and transferability of property rights it has been pointed out that this is not always possible. Some resources such as the atmosphere cannot be allocated in this way. The importance of exclusivity and transferability have been underscored by considering case studies of common property resources. Studies of land-holdings in Tripolitania and oyster beds in the United States are consistent with the view that exclusive private property rights are more efficient than common ownership. However, studies of common pool resources such as lobster fisheries and on-shore oilfields demonstrate that the pursuit of private interest may be anti-social in that the common pool is 'over-fished'. In particular, studies of oilfield unitisation have demonstrated that overriding landowners' private property interests in the interest of providing an exclusive right to the management of oil extraction leads to a more efficient yield of oil. Finally, the discussion of the evolution of mineral law in Nevada has demonstrated the importance of economic factors in determining the nature of property rights and the law.

3 The Coase Theorem

In the preceding chapter it was argued that universality, exclusivity and transferability of property rights would enhance efficiency in the use of resources. However, it was also pointed out that in some instances the pursuit of individual self-interest in the use of one's own property (be it in fishing, or land with sub-surface oil deposits) could lead to inefficiency. This arises because of the existence of common pool resources (fish stocks, reservoirs of oil and gas). These are examples of conflicting property rights which suggests the need to qualify the prescriptions of the property rights theorists. This chapter focuses on another type of property rights conflict – that between adjacent property-owners – to illustrate one of the fundamental propositions of the law-and-economics literature: the *Coase theorem*. The Coase theorem is in fact an application of a more general principle: that exchange only takes place when it is beneficial to both parties. Although the Coase theorem will be presented in terms of conflicting uses of property in this chapter, later in the book it will be applied to other legal conflicts.

CONFLICTING USES OF PROPERTY

Consider the case of *Sturges* v. *Bridgman* which came before the English Chancery Division Court in 1879. The facts in this case are as follows. A confectioner in Wigmore Street, London, used two mortars and pestles in carrying out his business. They had been in position for 26 and 60 years

27

respectively. A doctor then occupied neighbouring premises in Wimpole Street. After a period of eight years the doctor built a consulting room at the bottom of his garden against the confectioner's premises. It was then found that the noise and vibration from the mortars and pestles made it difficult for the doctor to use the consulting room. (He could not sound chests or engage in any occupation which 'required thought and attention'.) There would seem to be no problem relating to the definition of property rights here. Both parties had exclusive and transferable rights to operate their business which happened to be incompatible.

In the language of economists there was an *externality*. The operations of the confectioner imposed *external costs* on the doctor in that the cost of producing his output (health care) was increased (e.g. by the cost of soundproofing his consulting room, or indeed moving it). Put another way, the output which could be produced with a given set of inputs was reduced when the confectioner used his equipment (in fact the doctor's output it would seem was reduced to zero). Notice that what is involved here is an *unintended* consequence of one activity on another activity. In some situations the unintended consequence might be beneficial, e.g. the siting of an orchard and an apiary on adjoining land could raise the output of each activity. The important point in the economist's eyes is that the unintended consequence, whether positive or negative, is not paid for: the apple grower gains the benefit of pollination without charge; the doctor suffers the noise without compensation. This is only so, of course, so long as custom or law does not provide for a remedy. It was to find one that Sturges and Bridgeman appeared before the Chancery Division in 1879.

In fact an injunction was granted preventing the confectioner from using his machinery. However, this converts the situation to one in which the doctor's activities imposed a cost on the confectioner. An externality still existed. The court had simply chosen who had to bear the burden. This illustrates an important fact about externalities or incompatibilities: they are reciprocal. There was no incompatibility before the consulting room was built. So who caused the problem? No one really *caused* it. It simply arose from one of the many interdependences that exist in any society.

It is a question of public policy as to how such incompatibilities should be handled. It seems on the face of it 'unfair' that the confectioner should bear the burden – after all a confectioner's business had been there for a long time. However common law judges are reluctant to accept 'coming to the nuisance' as a defence.

Traditionally economists have favoured taxation of harmful activities (such as pollution) as a means of deterring them, but this does not appear particularly relevant to *Sturges* v. *Bridgman* (anyway which activity is the harmful one?). Some might suggest a system of physical planning which would not allow the operation of mortars and pestles in the same area as doctors' surgeries. That would seem an excessively large (and costly) hammer to crack a small nut (particularly if the doctor is the only one affected by the noise).

Ronald Coase (1960) who raised these issues in his seminal paper 'The Problem of Social Cost' took a rather different view from that previously taken by economists. He pointed out that the court's decision could easily be modified if that would give rise to the 'efficient' solution. The doctor could waive his right if the confectioner was willing to pay him a sufficient sum of money (i) to compensate for the loss of income brought about by the confectioner's activity, or (ii) sufficient to soundproof the room, or (iii) move his premises. Under what circumstances would the confectioner be willing to do this? Only if his loss of income from ceasing activity was greater than the amount necessary to compensate the doctor. Either way this would result in resources flowing to their highest valued use. Efficiency would be achieved. Notice that this result is actually independent of the court's decision. Had the court refused to grant an injunction it would still have been possible for the doctor to 'bribe' the confectioner to reduce the noise to an acceptable level if the doctor valued the use more than the confectioner. He could compensate the confectioner by (i) paying his lost income, or (ii) paying for soundproofing, or (iii) paying the confectioner's costs of moving elsewhere *but* only so long as operating in that place under noise-free conditions was worth more to the doctor than the cost of at least one of these courses of action.

These possibilities may be examined by attaching some hypothetical numbers to the facts in *Sturges* v. *Bridgman*. These are presented in Table 3.1.

Table 3.1

| | Profits* after all operating costs | |
	Noise	No Noise
Doctor	0	1000
Confectioner	2000	0

Cost* of alternative courses of action	
Doctor moving	1600
Confectioner moving	2500
Installation of soundproofing	250

Note: *These figures may be taken as the annual equivalents of the capital sums involved.*

Given the numbers in Table 3.1 if the court (as it did) grants an injunction to the doctor prohibiting the confectioner's use of the mortars and pestles the confectioner loses £2000 in profits, and the doctor earns £1000.

(a) Consider the courses of action open to the confectioner: He could pay the doctor's removal expenses of £1600 and the doctor would earn £1000 (by operating elsewhere) and the confectioner earn profits of £400. This is preferable to letting the injunction stand;

(b) the confectioner could consider moving but the cost would be greater than his potential profits and therefore he would not;

(c) the confectioner could install soundproofing thus reducing his profits to £1750 and the doctor would be as well off as with the injunction (i.e. making profits of £1000);

(d) the confectioner could pay the doctor £1000 compensation to cease practising leaving himself £1000 profit.

Given the injunction is in place the confectioner should choose (c) to maximise his profits and leave the doctor as well off as with the injunction.

What if the injunction had not been granted? The doctor

then loses £1000 profit and the confectioner gets £2000. A number of courses of action would still remain for the doctor:

(a) It's not worth the doctor's while to move since that would give him negative profits;

(b) paying the confectioner's moving expenses or compensating the confectioner would also result in losses to him;

(c) if the doctor paid for insulating the machines he would have profits of £750 and the confectioner £2000.

The doctor would serve his own best interest by choosing (c).

The important point to note here is that the same effect on resource allocation is achieved regardless of for whom the court finds. In either case both the doctor and the confectioner would continue to operate and £250 worth of insulation would be installed. Furthermore, regardless of how the court finds, the sum of the confectioner's and the doctor's profits is £2750. What the court's ruling decides is how the £2750 will be divided between the doctor and the confectioner. With the injunction it is in the ratio 1000:1750; without the injunction it is 750:2000. *If both parties behave rationally liability only determines the distribution of profits, it does not affect the allocation of resources.* Thus we might conclude (as Coase does) that when *costless* bargaining can take place the efficient solution is obtained regardless of upon whom the law imposes liability. This has become known as the *Coase Theorem*.

The qualification of costless bargaining is important. If bargaining absorbed resources in a significant amount the outcome might not be independent of the court's decision. Say it cost each party £1000 to arrive at a negotiated decision. Granted the injunction, the doctor would not wish to negotiate unless the confectioner paid his negotiating costs, but the confectioner only stands to gain £1750 and therefore the injunction stands and only the doctor operates. If the injunction is not granted the doctor will not find negotiations profitable and consequently the confectioner operates and the doctor does not.

The cost of bargaining is one aspect of what economists call *transaction costs*. These include the cost of finding transactors, negotiating the transaction and policing and enforcing its terms.

The Coase theorem is usually expressed as follows: 'When transaction costs are zero the allocation of resources is independent of the distribution of property rights.' This is often referred to as the *neutrality version* of the Coase theorem since it stresses the conclusion that the state of the law does not determine the *composition* of output. In our version of *Sturges* v. *Bridgman* the output of confectionery and health care was independent of whether the doctor had a right to a noiseless, vibration-free, environment or not (provided transaction costs were zero).

THE ASSUMPTIONS UNDERLYING THE COASE THEOREM

Implicit in the Coase theorem, as expressed above, are a number of assumptions; one of which we have made explicit: zero transaction costs. Cento Veljanovski (1982) lists a number of other implicit assumptions:

(a)   What he calls *Smith's proposition*: that voluntary exchange is mutually beneficial;
(b)   perfect knowledge, including knowledge of production, profit or utility functions. (Veljanovski says that this implies *no strategic behaviour*);
(c)   competitive markets;
(d)   costless court system;
(e)   producers maximise profit and consumers maximise utility;
(f)   there are no wealth effects.

Strategic behaviour is really another source of transaction costs that can arise under uncertainty. Similarly, a court system that uses up resources is also a transaction cost. (The economist's definition of costs as opportunity costs will be discussed in the next chapter.)

In what remains of this chapter the impact of relaxing two of these assumptions – no wealth effects, and the absence of strategic behaviour – will be discussed.

Wealth Effects
The question of wealth effects has been referred to by Kennedy

(1981) and Veljanovski (1982) as 'the ask/offer problem'. This is because it relates to different answers that might be received when posing two alternative questions to a single individual:

(a) How much money would you be prepared to offer to be free of this externality?

(b) How much money would you be willing to accept as compensation for putting up with this externality?

Both answers are lump-sums: that to (a) will be the maximum someone is prepared to pay; whilst that to (b) the minimum he will accept. The distinction between the two is relevant to our discussion of the Coase theorem because the allocation of entitlements by a court will determine which one is relevant to an individual in a particular case in order to establish his loss or gain in welfare from the court's decision.

Consider the classic economic case of an externality: smoke from a factory chimney polluting the atmosphere and making it more difficult to keep clothes on the washing-line clean. If the householder has no entitlement to a pollution-free atmosphere our measure of the impact of the externality is his answer to question (a). Clearly, he will only be willing to pay a sum of money that will leave him no worse off than he would be *with* the pollution.

In the absence of pollution he will attain some level of welfare (utility or happiness). Let us call this level A. With pollution his level of welfare is lower, say level B, which will be measured by the consumer's surplus he attains when the environment is polluted. Clearly, he would not be willing to give up a money amount greater than B to attain a pollution-free environment since that would give him a lower level of welfare without pollution than he could attain with pollution. Thus the maximum sum that could be extracted from him to avoid suffering the pollution is $A-B$. The lump sum of money equal to $A-B$ is called by economists the *equivalent variation in income* (EV).

If, on the other hand, the householder does have a right to a pollution-free environment, the factory owner might be willing to pay him to bear the pollution. How much would have to be paid is the answer to question (b) above. It will be the lump-sum equivalent to the loss suffered in going from the pollution-free environment to the polluted environment. It is the amount of money necessary to maintain the householder's welfare at level *A* when pollution takes place. This is called the *compensating variation in income* (CV) by economists. There is no reason to suppose that these two measures will be exactly the same. Economic theory suggests they will differ because of what are known as income (or wealth) effects. However theoretical calculations suggest that the difference will be so small as to be of no practical significance.

An intuitive understanding of why there should be a difference between the CV and EV is given by the following statement by Ezra Mishan (1967):

the maximum sum [a person] will pay for something valuable is obviously related to, indeed limited by, a person's total resources, while the minimum sum he is willing to accept for parting with these resources is subject to no such constraints.

Or to use Duncan Kennedy's (1981) example: How much is a house with a market value of $50,000 worth to you? If you already own the house you will require someone to pay you at least $50,000 for you to give it up (EV). If you don't own it and are relatively poor you would only be willing to pay much less than $50,000 to acquire it (CV) although if somehow your wealth were increased gradually you might eventually be willing to pay $50,000 for the house. Seen this way, a property right or entitlement is a form of wealth. Thus to whom the court gives protection affects the valuation that the individual will place on the right.

Our version of *Sturges* v. *Bridgman* did not give rise to this problem because we were dealing with two producers and the nuisance could be removed by installing insulation: it was symmetrical. The ask/offer problem only arises where consumption is involved (see Baker, 1975). This, however, will be very important since many externalities involve consumers. Should there be a significant difference between the two valuations the law would not have a neutral effect on resource allocation.

Economic theorists have concluded that wealth effects will be very small even for large changes in wealth (see Henderson, 1941; and Hicks, 1943). However a number of empirical studies discussed by Jack Knetsch (1983) and experiments reported in Knetsch and Sinden (1984) cast some doubt on the confidence with which economists dismiss the ask/offer distinction as an approximation. Knetsch reports a series of survey studies where people were asked to state how much they would be willing to pay to retain some environmental good which they currently enjoyed (e.g. wetlands for duck hunting, favourite fishing site, fishing pier, protection from air pollution) and how much they would require as compensation for forgoing it. The latter value was 2.3 to 16 times greater than the former. It should be noted that the sums of money involved here were small relative to the individuals' incomes, therefore there could be no income effect.

Economists are usually very sceptical of such surveys and hypothetical situations and have therefore tended to dismiss these results. Knetsch and Sinden, however, have conducted experiments using lottery tickets with groups of students and offers to buy the tickets back or demands for payment to retain the tickets. More people refused the compensation offer than paid to retain their tickets. In one experiment they were able to estimate the average willingness to pay to retain the ticket and the average compensation required to forgo the ticket. The latter was roughly four times the former. This evidence questions the validity of the neutrality version of the Coase theorem even in a transaction cost-free world.

Even if this problem could be neglected there is still the distributional consequence of any property rights decision. As we saw in *Sturges* v. *Bridgman*, although the efficient allocation of resources is attained regardless of the initial assignment, that assignment does affect the distribution (in this case of profits) between the parties. Society may not be indifferent to such distributional questions. The usual economist's answer is that the distributional consequences if undesirable can be dealt with by specific policies and not by interfering in the market. But here we are talking about an entitlement question which will determine how the market will operate. It is therefore not so easy to dodge.

Strategic Behaviour

A second assumption implicit in the Coase theorem is that

there is not strategic behaviour or, to put it another way: bargaining is cooperative. Given the way that transaction costs have been defined above (the costs of finding transactors, negotiating the transaction and policing and enforcing it) strategic behaviour may be seen as simply raising the costs of reaching a negotiated solution. However, strategic behaviour does have implications beyond this and it is therefore worth dealing with separately.

Above, the neutrality version of the Coase theorem was discussed. A second version (or interpretation) is what has been called the *bargaining version* (see Regan 1972; Cooter, 1982; Veljanovski, 1982). It is that bargaining between the parties will produce an efficient solution. This implicitly assumes that both parties to the bargain have the objective of maximising the joint welfare of the parties, i.e. they are playing a cooperative game. This is an implicit assumption in much standard economic analysis. However, it is somewhat in conflict with another assumption that economic agents are utility- or profit-maximisers. If each wants to maximise *his* utility or profit, why should he cooperate?

Standard economic theory tends to assume that all economic agents are gentlemen: they don't con or bluff people. It is much more realistic to assume some degree of strategic behaviour. The consequence of assuming this, however, may well be that the final bargain (if one is reached) will not be the best that can be obtained.

Consider the following hypothetical situation involving Burns and Baker, both of whom wish to foster a reputation as tough bargainers. The matrix in Table 3.2 shows the outcomes that will result when different strategies are adopted by Burns and Baker and each knows the pay-offs. The entries show on the left, the pay-off to Burns; and on the right, the pay-off to Baker for each of the combinations of strategies. Assume that each has to adopt one of two strategies: tough and weak.

Consider Burns' options: If he plays it tough he will gain either 3 or 10 depending on Baker's strategy. If he plays it weak he gets zero or 6 depending on Baker's strategy. But whatever strategy Baker plays Burns is better off if he plays it tough (i.e. 3/0 if Baker plays tough; or 10/6 if Baker plays it weak so he will play it tough).

Table 3.2

		Baker Tough	Weak
Burns	Tough	3,3	10,0
	Weak	0,10	6,6

Consider Baker's options: whichever strategy Burns adopts Baker does better if he plays it tough (3/0 or 10/6). Therefore Baker plays it tough. Since they both play it tough they end up with 3 each whereas if they had both played it weak they would have ended up with 6 each, i.e. both playing it weak is optimal, but in the absence of certain knowledge as to the other's strategy self-interest dictates playing it tough.

The point of all of this is that strategic behaviour can prevent the optimal allocation being attained. Thus in bargaining around an injunction strategic behaviour may result in a failure to obtain an efficient or cooperative bargain. In our *Sturges* v. *Bridgman* case, it was implictly assumed that both parties knew the cost of installing insulation. If they did not, strategic behaviour could result. For example, only the confectioner might know the cost of insulating the machine to be £250. He might wish to enhance his reputation as a hard bargainer in a situation where the injunction is not granted. Say he opened the bargaining by saying that it will cost £1000 to insulate the machine. This is equal to the total profits that the doctor can make so he might be unwilling to pay it. He finds out that for £400 he can soundproof the wall, therefore he rejects the bargain and spends £400 on insulation. The outcome is not as good as would be obtained by cooperative bargaining since it involves £600 profit for the doctor as opposed to £750. It also involves £400 of resources in soundproofing as opposed to £250 on insulation.

A number of writers have raised question-marks over the Coase theorem because of this type of problem. Whether the problem is significant or not is essentially empirical. What happens in the real world? The nearest we can come to an answer to this is a series of experiments reported by Hoffman and Spitzer (1982; 1986) and Harrison and McKee (1985).

In a carefully constructed experiment Hoffman and Spitzer presented pairs of people with information on pay-offs that each would receive if one of them (designated controller) chose a number from the list. The controller can be seen to be analogous to someone awarded an entitlement by a court. The numbers were chosen so that the Pareto-optimal choice involved some bargaining. Some of the experimental conditions were varied to produce repeated games to see if the existence of a continuing relationship between the parties affected outcomes. Also some situations were created where each party only knew how much he/she would get depending on the number chosen but not what the other would get, although they were permitted to disclose how much they would get. The game was also played with three parties and the possibility of joint controllers. This mimicked the situation of a polluter and two households where the households were granted injunctions. In almost 90 per cent of the trials and optimal choice was made. The only deviations from it occurred when there were three parties, joint controllers and each party only knew information concerning his/her pay-off.

The authors conclude that their results. provide strong support for Coase's (implied) proposition that agents will bargain to a joint profit-maximising solution when it exists in two- and three-party bargaining under full information and when one party has the right to make decisions under limited information. The results of the three-person, jointly controlled, partial information experiments are not clear-cut because some of the departures from optimality did not occur in later stages of repeated games. Furthermore, as Harrison and McKee (1985) point out, one aspect of Hoffman and Spitzer's (1982) results is not wholly consistent with the underpinnings of the Coase theorem. In a significant number of experiments whilst the parties negotiated the optimal outcome the division of the benefits between the parties was not individually rational. In many of these cases the benefits were divided equally between the parties when this left the controller worse off than he would have been had an agreed division not been reached. Harrison and McKee conducted a number of experiments which supported the view that the deviations from the Coasian result in Hoffman and Spitzer's experiments was due to the relative insignificance of the sums of money involved. These experiments do not give much information on the contention that as the number of parties to a bargain rise significantly optimal bargains fail to occur. It is usually argued that transaction costs become significant when 'many' bargainers are involved but no one has suggested how many are 'many'. It is typically argued that if, say, there are a large number of victims of pollution (e.g. households, the public at large) and a single polluter or (indeed) many polluters the Coase theorem will break down because of 'free-rider' or 'hold-out' problems. However, more recent evidence from experiments reported by Hoffman and Spitzer (1986) suggests considerable robustness in the Coase theorem's predictions for groups of up to 19 individuals. In addition these latest experiments consider the means by which the experimenters allocate 'property rights' between subjects. It was found less likely that deviating from optimality would occur where the subject had 'earned' the property right rather than acquired it by chance. The implication was that subjects who had acquired the 'property right' in the experiment by chance did not feel 'entitled' to it and therefore did not bargain in the way in which they would in a non-experimental situation.

All of these experiments suggest that the Coase theorem may be fairly robust in large-number situations. Experimental effects cannot, of couse, be ruled out. It should also be noted that in these experiments other transaction costs are low. In real life it may be the existence of these other transaction costs which lead to breakdown.

SUMMARY

In this chapter one of the most fundamental propositions in the law-and-economics literature (the Coase theorem) has been outlined and illustrated by the facts of the nuisance case *Sturges* v. *Bridgman*. The implications of the Coase theorem for the impact of judicial decisions on the allocation of resources has been discussed and significance of the assumptions of no wealth effects and no strategic behaviour for Coase's analysis outlined.

Experimental evidence on the significance of these assumptions was discussed. These suggest that while wealth effects arising from property rights allocation may generate asymmetry, strategic behaviour may be less of a problem than might be though *a priori*. A third assumption, a costless court system, has so far been passed over without comment. Superficially it would seem improbable. Clearly the courts use up resources in their operation. However, not all conflicts reach the courts. Well-defined principles of property and tort law are likely to mean that the court's decision can be anticipated with some certainty and bargaining takes place. Only in marginal cases will the court system be used. Another way of looking at this is to see that the law in many instances represents an overhead or fixed cost that does not affect efficiency in every particular bargain. Nevertheless, in marginal cases the cost of using the courts may be a considerable blockage to optimality.

The way in which society and in particular the courts should handle disputes in which transaction costs are not trivial has been a major concern of the law-and-economics literature. The analysis of this question will be the concern of Part II of this book where the focus is the law itself.

4 Economic Efficiency

Two versions (or interpretations) of the Coase theorem were discussed in the previous chapter: the neutrality version and the bargaining version. In this chapter we discuss a third version which from the economist's perspective is perhaps the most fundamental. This is the so-called *efficiency version* which concludes that in the absence of transaction costs an efficient allocation of resources will be attained regardless of which party is assigned the entitlement by the court. In the two preceding chapters the terms efficiency and optimality have been used without providing a formal definition. In this chapter concepts such as efficiency are explored in more detail, for their meaning and significance is of crucial importance in Part II of this book where legal doctrines are examined from an economic perspective. This chapter sets out to explain the fundamental economic concepts used in the law-and-economics literature. As such it may be omitted by those readers who are familiar with welfare economics.

PARETO OPTIMALITY

Much of law-and-economics scholarship is concerned with *allocative efficiency*. Can the current allocation of resources between competing uses be improved upon? How is it affected by the law? The fundamental question here is how we might define an improvement – an improvement for whom?

The definition of an efficient allocation of resources most commonly used by economists is known as the *Pareto*

41

criterion, after the Italian sociologist Vilfredo Pareto. According to the Pareto criterion an allocation of resources is efficient if it is not possible to reallocate resources in such a way that *at least* one person is better off (in his/her own judgement) and no one else is worse off (in his/her own judgement). Such an efficient allocation of resources is said to be *Pareto optimal.*

There are a number of points which should be noted about this definition of efficiency:

(a)   The criterion is *not value-free*. Most economists accept that it is based on value judgements but would argue that they are 'widely accepted' or 'almost non-controversial'. The value-judgements are:
   (i)   concern is with the welfare of individuals: society does not exist independently of the individuals who make it up (methodological individualism); thus social welfare is but the welfare of the individuals in a given society.
   (ii)   the individual is the best judge of his/her own welfare.

What has been referred to, here, as the Pareto criterion is sometimes referred to as *the* Paretian value-judgement.

(b)   the Pareto criterion is highly conservative. The way in which it has been expressed above may seem relatively uncontroversial but consider it further. As compared with the *status quo ante*, if a reallocation of resources will make one person better off and no one worse off, the reallocation may be said to be Pareto *superior* to the *status quo ante*. This may be called the weak version of the Pareto criterion. Consider a *stronger*, negative, version of the criterion. A reallocation of resources which makes one person worse off (in their own judgement) is *not* a Pareto improvement and should not be made. Even if the person made worse off is *very rich* and is made only marginally worse off and all those made better off are very poor such a reallocation fails the Pareto criterion. The Pareto criterion is very conservative because very few reallocations will satisfy it. It is biased towards the *status quo*.

It is worth stressing the distinction between *Pareto optimality* and *Pareto superiority*. The fact that a given allocation of resources is Pareto optimal does *not* mean that it is Pareto superior to all other allocations. Some of these other allocations may themselves be Pareto optimal. Consider an example: Kate and Lucy's father has a box containing 100 Smarties. Under allocation I, he gives Kate 60 and Lucy 40. I is Pareto superior to the initial position since both Kate and Lucy are made better off (since both like Smarties and let us assume that the father does not). Under allocation II, he gives Kate 40 and Lucy 60. II is also Pareto superior to the initial position since both girls are better off under allocation II than they were initially. However, if the move to I is actually made no move that takes Smarties away from one child and gives them to the other is Pareto superior to allocation I and we might conclude that allocation I is Pareto optimal (at least with respect to the allocation of Smarties). On the other hand, if the move was initially made to allocation II that allocation may be said to be Pareto optimal since no reallocation of Smarties can make one child better off without making the other worse off. thus both I and II are Pareto optimal allocations but neither is Pareto superior to the other.

Notice that there are a very large number of possible ways of allocating the Smarties initially, each of which will be Pareto optimal but none of which is Pareto superior to the others. This is not to say that every possible allocation is Pareto optimal. If allocation III involves giving Kate 40 Smarties and Lucy 50 Smarties it is not Pareto optimal because allocation IV, which gives Kate 50 and Lucy 50, is Pareto superior: Kate is better off and Lucy is no worse off than under III. It can also be seen why III might be termed inefficient: it can be improved upon because it leaves some resources (Smarties) unused.

Notice that if a further value-judgement about the relative deservingness of Kate and Lucy is added, an allocation which would be superior to all others could be found, e.g. if the father judges that they are equally deserving the optimal solution is to give them 50 Smarties each. Economists would talk about this as imposing a social welfare function which has a preference for egalitarian distributions. On the other hand, if the father is unwise he might give one of them twice the weight of the other in his social welfare function and give 2/3 of the box to one and 1/3 to the other. This distribution would maximise welfare, *given* the father's imposed social welfare function. The point here is that a single optimum (or *optimum optimorum*) can only be attained by making value-judgements as to the relative deservingness of the members of society. The Pareto criterion resists doing that and thus leaves us unable to choose between an infinite number of Pareto optimal allocations. It also might be interpreted as meaning that the existing distribution of resources (so long as it involves no waste) seems always to be optimal. But this is not so, because only one resource (Smarties) has been considered. The picture changes when a second resource is introduced.

Consider two resources – Smarties and Spangles – so long as the two children do not value both kinds of sweets similarly any distribution the father makes *may* be improved upon by the children exchanging the sweets between themselves. If he gives each 50 Smarties and 40 Spangles (exhausting his supply) and Kate values 2 Smarties at 1 Spangle and Lucy 1 Smartie to 1 Spangle, then Kate would be willing to give up 2 Smarties in exchange for 1 Spangle and feel no worse off. If Lucy received 2 Smarties in exchange for 1 Spangle she would feel better off. Therefore an allocation of 48 Smarties and 41 Spangles to Kate and 52 Smarties and 39 Spangles to Lucy is Pareto superior to giving each 50 + 40. Such trading could continue until neither could benefit from trade. The resulting allocation would be Pareto optimal.

However, it is unlikely that as each child's holding of sweets changed that the exchange rate which they would be willing to trade at would be constant. As Kate's number of Smarties fell she would be likely to value Smarties more highly. Economists call this the *diminishing rate of marginal substitution in consumption*.

Note also that the father needs no knowledge of the relative values which each child places on the two kinds of sweet in order for a Pareto optimal allocation to be reached. The initial distribution (50 + 40) which was not optimal was improved upon by trade without any interpersonal comparisons being made by the father.

However, which of the many Pareto optimal allocations is

eventually reached will be determined by the initial distribution. Corresponding to each initial distribution of resources there will be a Pareto optimal allocation of resources that can be reached by trade. But in the absence of a social welfare function there is nothing to choose between the different Pareto optimal allocations given the endowment of resources.

In the course of illustrating the Pareto criterion we have demonstrated another principle dear to economists and implicit in the Coase theorem: free exchange or trade can improve welfare. This lies behind the economists support of competitive markets.

THE EFFICIENCY VERSION OF THE COASE THEOREM

The meaning of the efficiency version of the Coase theorem should now be obvious. In terms of the hypothetical arithmetic attributed to *Sturges* v. *Bridgman* in Chapter 3, regardless of the courts finding the outcome assuming costless negotiation, i.e. trading, will be that the doctor would continue to practise, the confectioner would continue to produce and £250 of insulation would be used. There is no reallocation of resources from medical practice, confectionery manufacture and insulation that can be attained without making the doctor or the confectioner or *both* worse off. In other words, if the assumptions underlying the Coase theorem hold, an efficient allocation of resources will be achieved regardless of the initial distribution of property rights.

For the negotiation (or trading) to take place, however, the court must give somebody the property rights. Who gets the right does not affect the *allocation of resources* but does affect the *distribution of the benefits* from the trading between the doctor and the confectioner (just as the initial distribution of Smarties and Spangles affected the final distribution between Kate and Lucy).

Let us also return to the hypothetical arithmetic of *Sturges* v. *Bridgman* to see yet another interesting result.

If the injunction is granted we saw that the doctor made a

profit of £1000, the confectioner a profit of £1750 and £250 worth of insulation was purchased. The aggregate profits of both parties was £2750. On the other hand, if the injunction was refused the doctor made a profit of £750, the confectioner £2000 and £250 worth of insulation was purchased. Aggregate profits was again £2750, i.e. not only was the allocation of resources the same in that the same level of resources was devoted to health care, confectionery and insulation but the same aggregate profits were made. The difference between the effects of the two judgments was how those profits were distributed between the doctor and the confectioner. Either way the Pareto optimal allocation of resources will be attained.

ECONOMIC PROFITS AND PRODUCERS' SURPLUS

The discussion so far has been fairly imprecise as to what is meant by profits. Most non-economists will have a working definition of profits: the difference between revenue received by a firm and the costs it incurs in producing that revenue. Economists, however, have a more technical definition of profits. In order to keep clear in our minds the distinction between this concept of profits and the layman's concept we use the term *economic profit* for the economist's definition. Economic profit is the difference between a firm's total revenue and the total *opportunity cost* of the resources used to produce that revenue. The opportunity cost of a resource is its value in its next best use. It is not just financial cost: even if a firm is not paying rent for its premises it still incurs an opportunity cost if it uses them; it could always rent them out to someone else.

Say Mr Jones owns a field which he inherited from his father. He pays no rent for it and grazes two cows on it. He sells the cows' milk for £200 p.a. and feeding the cows, etc. costs him £150 p.a. On the layman's definition of profit he makes £50 profit p.a. But what is the opportunity cost of the resources he uses? Let us say he could rent his field out to a nearby arable farmer for £100 p.a. Thus whilst the first farmer pays no rent for the field on which he grazes his cows he forgoes £100 p.a. in rent for the privilege of doing so, i.e. his *implicit* cost is £100. If this is the highest rent he could obtain it is the opportunity cost of the land. Thus the owner of the land should charge himself £100 p.a. for using the field. We can see right away that this converts the profit of £50 (200–150) to a loss of £50 (200–(150+100)). This is without considering the opportunity cost of the farmer's time (what he could earn in another occupation in the time he spends looking after the cows) or the capital he has tied up in the two cows. In the latter case let us say he could sell the two cows for £100 and put the proceeds in a bank account earning 10 per cent p.a. (or £10 p.a.). Thus the opportunity cost of having capital tied up in the cattle is £10 p.a. That should be seen as a cost to the farmer. Notice that if he could find another way of investing that £100 which earned him more than £10 p.a. – say £12 – then the opportunity cost would be £12. Opportunity cost is the *highest valued* alternative use.

The amount of interest that could be earned by investing money in a bank account is often taken as the opportunity cost of capital because that is a guaranteed return – it is risk-free and requires no special investment skills. A safe, risk-free, investment might be considered to be the purchase of government bonds. This is often what is implied when economists talk of *the* rate of interest, i.e. the rate of interest earned on government bonds. Note that since we have taken the opportunity cost of the field to be £100 p.a. that must be greater than could be earned by selling the field and investing the proceeds of the sale at the rate of interest.

Returning to our farmer, it can be seen that using the field to graze two cows has significant opportunity costs which are more than enough to convert the £50 profit into an *economic loss* (negative economic profit).

To summarise: the economist's concept of cost is opportunity cost: what could be earned in the best alternative use for the resources. A rational economic agent will seek to maximise the difference between total revenue and total opportunity cost, i.e. economic profit. Since the economic concept of cost is opportunity cost, maximising profit implies that resources are being used in their most highly valued use. Opportunity costing ensures that resources are costed on a common basis whatever their current use. Maximising the difference between the revenue gained from selling what they produce and their opportunity cost will mean they are being used in their most valuable use. Provided the market in which the product is sold is competitive maximising profits will result in efficiency.

Economists usually assume that the opportunity cost of the resources used to produce a good will rise as the quantity of the good produced rises. This is because the more of the good that is produced the more resources will be required and the more attractive will be their alternative use. We can therefore think of a graph of opportunity cost as rising as more of the good is produced, as in Figure 4.1.

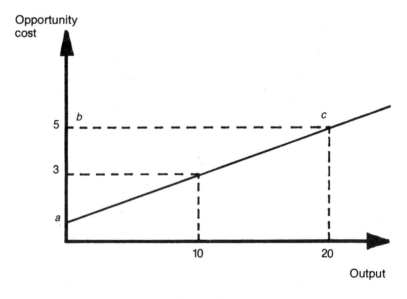

Figure 4.1

Since opportunity cost is the value of these resources in their alternative use, it is the *minimum* value the output must be sold for to make it worthwhile producing, i.e. the minimum price required to cover opportunity cost of producing that unit. This opportunity cost curve is what economists call the supply curve of the good. For each level of output of the good it tells us what the price must be for it to be worthwhile producing the last unit.

The supply curve is also the marginal cost curve because its height tells us the cost of producing one more (or the marginal) unit of the good. If the individual producer has no control over price (i.e. it is exogenously determined) then he will produce up to the point where price = opportunity cost or marginal cost of a unit. The total opportunity cost of resources used is the area below the supply curve. If price is 5 and therefore output is 20, then total revenue is 5 × 20 and economic profit is 100 minus the area under supply curve, i.e. the area of *abc*. This triangle is also known as *producers' surplus* or *economic rent*. It is the surplus over and above that necessary to attract the resources to that particular use. Maximising profit maximises producers' surplus and will result in the output for which $p = mc$ being produced (if the market is competitive). Thus an efficient allocation of resources will be one for which $p = mc$, i.e. the price paid for each unit of the good produced will be equal to the opportunity cost of the resources used in producing *the last unit* of the good produced.

Returning to *Sturges* v. *Bridgman*: if confectionery and medicine are competitively produced each party will maximise profits (and producers' surplus) by producing up to the point where $p = mc$, i.e. opportunity cost of producing the last unit of the good. The output at which this occurs is unaffected by who bears the cost of the insulation. This is because the cost of the insulation is not a marginal cost: it is not a function of output. If the doctor is granted the injunction the confectioner spends £250 on insulation whether he produces 1 or 1000 units of confectionery. It reduces the confectioner's profit but not the output at which that profit is maximised. Conversely, if the injunction is not granted the doctor's profit is reduced. The insulation cost is a fixed or overhead cost and this does not affect the marginal cost of production.

CONSUMERS' SURPLUS

The preceding section concerned producers' surplus and profit. This section considers consumers' surplus. The analogue to the supply curve is the *demand* curve. It is normally assumed that the demand curve is downward sloping: as the price of a good falls, all other things being equal, more of it will be consumed. (All other things include tastes, incomes, prices of other goods, etc.)

What does the price of a good represent from the consumer's point of view? He or she gives up the power to obtain other goods. If good A costs £10 that £10 is no longer available to buy goods B, C, D ... etc. The cost of A is really the units of other goods given up to attain it: that is, the opportunity cost of A.

Why should the consumer choose A rather than B or C or D, etc.? Economists usually argue that what consumers want is not good A but the utility or satisfaction they derive from consuming A. Consequently, if a consumer chooses A when B or C is available the utility obtained from consuming A must be greater than the utility or satisfaction to be obtained from spending the same amount of money on any other combination of goods. A point on a demand curve can be seen as the maximum price per unit consumers are willing to pay to obtain that unit of the good and must therefore be a proxy for the utility derived from consuming that good.

Looked at from the point of view of the individual consumer it is usually argued that the more one consumes, the less additional satisfaction (marginal utility) one will obtain from consuming an extra unit. Therefore the price one is willing to pay for extra units will fall, i.e. the individual demand curve slopes down to the right (it is negatively sloped). When aggregated over all consumers this analysis produces a market demand curve such as that illustrated in Figure 4.2.

At price P_1 only consumers who value the good highly will be willing to forgo the other goods on which P_1 could be spent. As price falls consumers who value the good less will now find it worth buying. If the price falls to P_2, Q_2 units will be consumed. Since all consumers will pay the same unit price in a competitive market those who would have consumed Q_1 units at P_1 now get them for less (P_2): they pay less than they would have been willing to. They have to give up less of other goods; but they still get the same satisfaction from them. Consequently, the price they pay no longer represents the

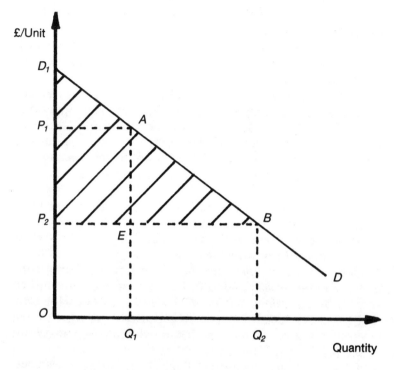

Figure 4.2

utility which they obtain. They obtain what economists call *consumers' surplus*. The true value of the good to them is not its price but what they would have willingly paid (P_1). For the individual who consumes the $Q_1 th$ unit at P_2 who would have paid P_1 to obtain it the consumers' surplus is ($P_1 - P_2$).

Notice, that at price P_2 not only do the consumers of the Q_1 units obtain consumer surplus but every consumer who buys the good other than the consumer of the Q_2th unit (who actually values it just at P_2). He is the marginal consumer. All the intra-marginal consumers obtain consumers' surplus. Notice that for the consumer of the Q_2th unit its consumption yields him utility equal to the price of the good i.e. the value of the last unit to society equals its price.

Aggregate consumers' surplus for a good is thus represented by the area between the demand curve and the market price. In terms of Figure 4.2 then P_2D_2B represents the difference between what the consumers of the Q_2 units of the good would be willing to pay (OD_1BQ_2) and what they actually have to pay (OP_2BQ_2). It is the *net* benefit the consumers obtain from purchasing and consuming the good.

If for some reason the price of the good to consumers rose (say by the introduction of a tax or because supply was reduced) to P_1 only Q_1 units would be purchased. How does this affect the previous consumers of the Q_2 units? Those who previously consumed Units Q_1 to D_2 no longer consume the good. They are clearly worse off, but by how much? Their willingness to pay for the good was Q_1ABQ_2 but they now have Q_1EBQ_2 ($P_2 \times (Q_2 - Q_1)$) available to spend on other things. What they have actually lost is the consumers' surplus on these units of the good, i.e. *EAB*. This triangle is often referred to as the *deadweight loss*.

Those who still consume the Q_1 are also affected. The increase in purchase price to P_1 has reduced their consumers' surplus by the amount P_2P_1AE (i.e. $(P_1 - P_2)Q_1$). However, that is not a deadweight loss because it accrues to the government, if it is an increase due to reduced supply it accrues to the producers. Either way it is not a loss to society but a *transfer* from some members of society to others. Unless we are prepared to comment on the relative deservingness of consumers and those who benefit from the transfer (which most economists are not willing to do) nothing can be said about it in terms of economic welfare. Therefore the net effect of the price rise is the deadweight loss. This is the measure of the loss of economic welfare occasioned by the change in price to the consumer.

Consumer surplus is therefore a measure of economic welfare. In the preceding section it was seen that from the producer's side, producers' surplus is also a measure of economic welfare. The two are brought together by bringing together the demand curve and the supply curve for the good as in Figure 4.3.

The market-determined price is that where the supply and demand curves intersect, P_E. At that price consumers' surplus is P_EBE and producers' surplus is AP_EE. Their sum, ABE, is a measure of the net benefit of producing Q_E units of the good.

No other output can generate a sum of consumers' and producers' surplus greater than this. If output is lower, say Q_1, there is a loss of *FCE* (*DCE* consumers' surplus and *FDE* producers' surplus) leaving *ABCF*. Note that the balance between consumers' and producers' surplus also changes.

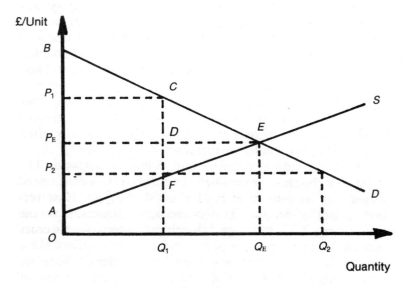

Figure 4.3

Outputs greater than Q_E, say Q_2, would generate higher consumers' surplus but this would be more than outweighed by the loss of producers' surplus because price would be less than the cost of some of the inputs. Output Q_E is the efficient output of this good since no one can be made better off without someone being made worse off.

In the preceding section it was demonstrated that for the last unit of the good produced price equals marginal cost. In this section viewing it from the consumption side the value of the last unit produced to the consumer, also, equalled price. Therefore at the equilibrium market price the value of the marginal unit (its marginal benefit) equals the marginal cost of producing it. Looking at things this way we can see the supply curve as a marginal cost of production curve and the demand curve as the marginal benefit of production curve. Equilibrium price and output are attained where the marginal benefit of production equals the marginal cost of production. Mathematically speaking this is the first-order condition for maximising the sum of consumers' surplus and producers' surplus. It is therefore the condition which must be met for economic efficiency to be attained in the production and consumption of this good.

Other conditions can be generated which link this condition across consumers to produce the conditions for the overall attainment of a Pareto optimum. (it is not necessary to go into the technical details of this here.)

Any restriction of output in an industry below that where price equals marginal cost therefore marginal benefit equals marginal cost reduces social welfare. A monopolist would find it in his interest to reduce output transforming some consumers' surplus into producers' surplus and therefore higher profits for him. This is inefficient because it would result in $p(= \mathrm{MB}) > MC$ and therefore the sum of producers' surplus and consumers' surplus would not be maximised. Thus the efficiency interpretation of the Coase theorem implies that in the absence of transactions costs the allocation of rights will not change the sum of consumers' and producers' surpluses.

The measure of consumer surplus used here is that due to the French economist Dupuit and the English economist Alfred Marshall. It is subject to one or two qualifications and should be replaced by measures devised by Sir John Hicks. However Hicks' measures are technically more complex. Since the gain in technical complexity does not change any of the implications relevant to the subject matter of this book the simple measure will be retained. Some qualifications to this (Marshallian) concept will however, be noted:

(i)   The concept of consumers' surplus used here was arrived at by considering a single good. It was implicitly assumed that when he consumed good A the consumer derived consumers' surplus but that he derived no consumer surplus from the alternative goods he forwent. Consequently all the consumers' surplus from the consumption of A was a net benefit. Had he derived some in the consumption of B then the benefit of consuming A would have been $CS_A - CS_B$. A consequence of this is that the deadweight loss from a price rise may be less than the area of the triangle. In fact the Marshallian analysis implicitly assumes that every consumer of A is the marginal consumer of his alternative choice.

(ii) No account has been taken of what happens in other markets as a consequence of the change in this market. For example, gains may accrue due to economies of scale being achieved by the higher demand for the alternative good.

(iii) It implicitly assumes that the marginal utility of income is constant for all individuals. The price an individual is willing to pay for a good represents the utility he derives from it. If the marginal utility of income is the same for all individuals then the rate at which utility transforms into monetary units is the same for all individuals. Thus if Mr A is willing to pay £10 for a theatre ticket and Ms B is willing only to pay £8 it can be deduced that Mr A derives more utility from having the ticket than Ms B. Consequently the welfare of society is higher by Mr A having the ticket. However most people would accept that the utility value of £1 of income is different for people on different income levels. At the extreme, an additional £1 to the millionaire will yield less utility than an additional £1 to a poor person. Thus if Mr A is very rich and Ms B very poor, the utility represented by Mr A's £10 could conceivably be less than that represented by Ms B's £8. Thus relative willingness to pay may not represent relative utility gains and consumers' surplus measured in money terms may not be the same as that in real terms for people with different incomes.

In spite of these qualifications regarding the measurement of consumers' surplus the main conclusion remains: social welfare will be maximised when the sum of consumers' and producers' surpluses is maximised. Such a position would be

Pareto optimal since a move from it must make someone worse off. However the converse is *not* true. The allocation of resources which maximises the surpluses is not Pareto superior to all other allocations since the move from the current position may make someone worse off, e.g. a move from a level of output produced by a monopolist to the higher output which would be produced under competition might fail the Pareto criterion because the monopolist is made worse off, even though the gain in consumers' surplus is greater than the loss of producers' surplus. The move might be made voluntarily (and thus satisfy the Pareto criterion) if consumers gave up some of their potential gain in consumers' surplus to allow the monopolist to remain as well off as he was before, i.e. if the move was achieved by trading. However, transactions costs might preclude such traded gains from being achieved.

The next section of this chapter outlines a criterion of efficiency which some economists would use in preference to the Pareto criterion because it avoids these problems by using aggregate welfare rather than changes in individual welfare. This is the Kaldor-Hicks criterion which supplies the underpinning of the concept of efficiency used in much of the law-and-economics literature. Before turning to the Kaldor-Hicks criterion it is necessary to generalise the results of this section which has been conducted in terms of supply and demand curves and consumers' and producers' surpluses.

As has already been mentioned the supply curve is a *marginal cost* of production curve and the demand curve a *marginal benefit* of production curve. The optimum is achieved where the curves intersect and marginal benefit of production equals marginal cost of production. Production is only one of many forms of activity which utilises resources and these results may be generalised to all activities: the optimum resources will be devoted to an activity where the marginal social benefit of the activity equals the marginal social cost of the activity, i.e. $MSB = MSC$.

Above, it was noted that the $p = mc$ condition maximises the sum of producers' and consumers' surpluses. This is just the *net* benefit to society from production. Thus the condition $MSB = MSC$ maximises the net benefit from any activity. This general formulation is used by economists to analyse a great variety of policy problems (e.g. pollution, accidents, roads, bridges, etc.). It is a paradigm for casting any problem in a manner susceptible to the tools of marginal analysis. Figure 4.4 illustrates the general proposition. AB is the marginal social benefit curve for the activity and CD is the marginal social cost curve for the activity. They measure the additional benefit (cost) of increasing the level of activity by one unit, at any given level of activity. The net benefit of the activity at any level L is the area between the two curves up to that level of activity. That net benefit is maximised at L_E where $MSB = MSC$. If the level of activity were L_1, $MSB > MSC$ and the net benefit is the area $ACFG < ACE$. Thus the activity should be increased to L_E. If $L > L_E$, say L_2 $MSB < MSC$ and the net benefit is $(ACE + L_E EJL_2 - L_E EHL_2)$ or $(ACE - EHJ)$. Thus the level of activity should be reduced to L_E to maximise net benefit. It should be noted that Figure 4.4 embodies the common economic assumption that the marginal cost of an activity rises as the level of the activity rises whilst the marginal benefit declines as the activity level rises. In many places in Part II of this book diagrams analagous to Figure 4.4 will be use to analyse legal doctrines.

The Kaldor-Hicks criterion will approve moves to welfare optima such as L_E. This criteria is derived from the work of Nikolas (later Lord) Kaldor (1939) and Sir John Hicks (1939; 1940).

THE KALDOR-HICKS CRITERION

The Kaldor-Hicks criterion is essentially one of a *potential* Pareto improvement. It may be expressed thus:

A proposal for a change in the economy should be undertaken if those who are made better off by it *could* so compensate those made worse off by it that the latter would be as well off as before the change (in their own eyes) and the former still be better off (in their own eyes).

However the criterion does not require that such 'compensation' actually be paid: it is a hypothetical compensation. If such compensation actually were paid no one would be worse

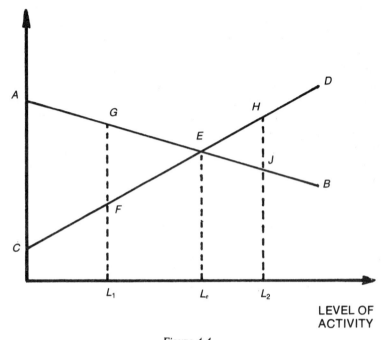

Figure 4.4

off but some better off and thus the change would satisfy the
Pareto criterion: hence the term *potential* Pareto improvement.

Kaldor, in proposing the criterion, argued that whether
compensation was paid or not was an ethical or political
question since it was about the distribution of income. What
the criterion established, according to Kaldor, is the effect of
the policy on production. Thus, it is claimed, the ethical and
economic evaluations of the policy may be separated.

The Kaldor-Hicks criterion has been identified as a criterion
of *wealth maximisation* (particularly in the law-and-economics
literature). It should really be understood in terms of the
subjective evaluations of the parties involved (i.e. changes in
their utilities). It therefore takes account of non-monetised
phenomena. The Kaldor-Hicks criterion would appear to be

much more widely satisfiable than the Pareto criterion since it only requires that the benefits from a policy should exceed the costs, not that there should be no negative effects. A considerable economics literature has grown around the criterion in which it has been subject to modification and qualification but these need not be considered for present purposes (see further Boadway and Bruce, 1984). The Kaldor-Hicks criterion is the basis of much applied welfare economics such as the use of Cost-Benefit Analyses of public policies. It is also the underpinning of much law-and-economics scholarship. The Coase Theorem may not be applicable to most real-world legal problems because transaction costs prevent efficient bargaining from taking place. Thus the assignment of property rights or entitlements will affect not only the distribution of the gains but the allocation of resources. What then would be the 'efficient' way to assign entitlements? The answer given by mainstream law-and-economics is encapsulated in what Veljanovski (1982) calls *Posner's Proposition:*

When market transaction costs are prohibitive, rights should be assigned to those who value them most.

Posner, himself, has identified this with the Kaldor-Hicks criterion. Under it the gainers would be able to compensate the loser *if* bargaining could take place. In such circumstances, then, regardless of the initial assignment, the property right would end up with those who gain most from having it. This would be the 'efficient' allocation. Efficiency therefore dictates a certain allocation of rights.

When transaction costs are high so that bargaining is *not* feasible the efficient allocation can only be obtained by a court (or some other public authority) assigning the right to the person who would have ended up with it had bargaining been feasible, i.e. the person who values it most.

Consider again the numerical example based on *Sturges* v. *Bridgman.* Remember in that example with zero transaction costs both the doctor and the confectioner produced and £250 worth of insulation was purchased. If transaction costs were high – say £1000 for each party – the optimal solution would not be achieved since negotiation is not profitable. Clearly in such circumstances the choice of initial entitlement may be important. If it is given to the doctor he produces and the confectioner does not: profits of £1000 are made. On the other hand, if it is given to the confectioner, he produces and the doctor does not: £2000 of profits are made.

If profits are representative of the value of the goods to society then the latter solution is the one which satisfies the Kaldor–Hicks criterion and the property right should be given to the confectioner since he could hypothetically compensate the doctor and still be better off than he would be if the entitlement had been given the other way. If this involved transferring the right from the doctor it would not satisfy the Pareto criterion. Had the entitlement been given to the doctor he would *not* have been able to compensate the confectioner and still be better off himself.

So far only choices *between* the two parties have been considered. The optimal solution results in both parties producing and insulation being purchased. Could the court (or other authority) attain that solution? It depends on the source of transaction costs. Say a negotiated solution is not attainable due to the strategic behaviour on the part of the confectioner. He overestimates the cost of insulating the machinery in order to extract a greater sum from the doctor. The efficient allocation could be obtained by giving the entitlement to the doctor. He could then produce and the confectioner would only produce if he could insulate at a cost less than his potential profits. The problem here is that the court would have to know that the machinery could be insulated at a cost less than the doctor's potential profits. On the other hand, if the court felt that the doctor could insulate himself for less than the confectioner could, it should give the entitlement to the confectioner thus encouraging the doctor to provide insulation at the lower cost.

In general, it might be expected that the producer of the noise could be the least-cost avoider of the harm and this might be seen as a justification of the usual rule of the courts to grant an injunction in favour of the plaintiff in that it would encourage the defendant to seek out the least-cost remedy (whether it involves him insulating himself, or insulating the plaintiff). Of course, where negotiation is possible it doesn't even matter if the court is wrong about who the least-cost avoider is. Negotiations will right its error (Coase Theorem). However, if strategic behaviour cannot be avoided once the entitlement is determined there is no guarantee that negotiation will produce the efficient outcome. Consider a case involving a noise-producing factory and a number of residents. Even where the profit which the factory could make exceeds the value of being free of noise to the residents, because there are so many of them, the cost of negotiation and the possibility of hold-out problems might mean that if the residents were granted an injunction it would not be worth the factory owner trying to buy them out. Conversely, if the injunction were not granted and the residents valued peace more than the factory's profits it might not be possible for the large number of residents to negotiate successfully among themselves to buy out the factory.

In either of these circumstances the efficient situation would not seem to be attainable. But this is due to our having considered only one way of protecting an entitlement – an injunction. The alternative means by which such disputes are resolved are the subject-matter of Part II of this book in which legal doctrines are examined from an economic perspective. The purpose of the present chapter has been to outline the economic concepts of efficiency and welfare optima. In the absence of an explicit social welfare function it has been argued that there are an infinite number of efficient allocations according to the Pareto criterion. Each Pareto optimum corresponds to a different initial distribution of resources. Under conditions of universal perfect competition the optima will be attained when in all markets price equals the marginal cost of production and consequently the sum of producers' and consumers' surpluses is maximised. In a world of non zero transactions costs the trading required to reach this optimum may not be feasible. Many economists would argue that in these circumstances the appropriate criteria for evaluating reallocations of resources is the Kaldor–Hicks criterion by which a reallocation is sanctioned if it is a potential Pareto improvement. Some contributors to the law-and economics literature have identified the Kaldor–Hicks criterion with

wealth-maximisation. It would be more accurate to identify it
with utility (or welfare)-maximisation.

DISTRIBUTIONAL CONSIDERATIONS

Thus far this chapter has been concerned exclusively with
efficiency. In passing it has been noted that different
entitlements may produce different allocations of resources
because they affect the wealth of individuals. It may be
possible to counteract the distributive consequences of
entitlement decisions via general redistributive policies but this
will not always be practicable. In spite of what most
economists write society may have distributional goals which it
rates *at least* as highly as efficiency. The Social Welfare
Function may be conceived as embodying distributive weights
reflecting social evaluations of relative deservingness. Both
efficiency and distribution should be considered together since
a given distributional goal may involve a sacrifice of efficiency
and conversely the attainment of efficiency may imply an unacceptable distribution of income.

In a world of zero transactions costs efficiency will be
obtained regardless of the initial allocation of entitlements.
Thus if distributional goals carry any weight in society the
initial entitlement should be that which comes closest to
achieving the distributional goals. Thus if the factory in the
earlier example is owned by a very rich person and the
residents are very poor then by granting an injunction in
favour of the residents the costs of installing filters will be
borne by the factory owner (in the form of reduced profits).
On the other hand, if the entitlement is given to the factory the
residents will bear the cost of the filters. Thus preference for a
more equalised distribution of income would suggest giving
the entitlement to the residents.

However, care is required here. The analysis of these
problems has been conducted using what economists call
partial equilibrium analysis: we have only been concerned with
the polluting activity and its direct consequences. We have not
explored the consequences of the decision for other parts of
the economy. What if the residents live in rented houses and

the removal of the pollution raises the value of property and allows the rich landlord to raise rents and acquire all the benefits of the court's decision? These higher rents may not even be paid by the original residents who perhaps cannot afford them. They may therefore move out and be replaced by other, richer tenants whose interests might not have weighed so heavily against those of the factory owner in the original decision.

Distributional considerations are likely to be even more important where the output of the 'nuisance'-creating firm will be affected by the court's decision. Reducing the output (perhaps to zero) will affect levels of employment and incomes of (possibly) relatively poor workers in the factory and the pollution conscious residents may in fact be relatively wealthy.

Incorporating distributional considerations in the analysis requires considerable care. Many economists would argue that it is not appropriate to economic analysis because it involves value-judgements. The counter to this is that to exclude distributional considerations equally implies a value-judgement that all agents should be treated as having the same weighting in the Social Welfare Function. Thus, in subsequent chapters both distributional and efficiency considerations will be examined.

Part II
Law

5 Entitlements and their Defence

Part II shifts the focus of this book from general economic principles to the economic analysis of specific legal doctrines and laws. Such analysis is by necessity selective. Relatively few areas of the law can be covered in the space available. However, before turning to these specific applications, this chapter elucidates a further set of concepts of general applicability which will be used in various places in subsequent chapters: the *property rule/liability rule* framework developed by Guido Calabresi and A. Douglas Melamed (1972). They argue that the process of legal adjudication involves, essentially, two stages:

> The first issue which must be faced by any legal system is one we call the problem of 'entitlement'. Whenever a state is presented with the conflicting interests of two to more people, or two or more groups of people, it must decide which side of favour. . . . Hence the fundamental thing that law does is to decide which of the conflicting parties will be entitled to prevail. The entitlement to make noise versus the entitlement to have silence, the entitlement to pollute versus the entitlement to breath clean air, the entitlement to have children versus the entitlement to forbid them – these are the first order of legal decisions . . .
>
> The state not only has to decide whom to entitle but it must also simultaneously make a series of equally difficult second order decisions. The decisions go to the manner in which entitlements are protected and to whether an individual is allowed to sell or trade the entitlement. (Calabresi and Melamed, 1972, pp.1090–2)

Entitlements are broadly similar to what have been referred to as property rights in Chapter 2. In effect, they cover all legal rights. 'Entitlement' probably conveys this general sense more effectively then the economist's term 'property right'. Henceforth the more general term will be used in this book. The discussion of the Coase Theorem in Chapter 3 and the examples built around the facts of *Sturges* v. *Bridgman* have implicitly assumed a simple legal remedy (the injunction) is available to protect an entitlement. However in Chapter 4 it was seen that in the presence of significant transaction costs such an approach could not guarantee an optimal outcome. It was somewhat cryptically stated there that this was because only one means of protecting an entitlement has been discussed. This chapter will be argued in terms of the effect which an activity carried out by one party (the injurer) has on another party (the victim). The nature of the activity is left non-specific because the objective of the present chapter is conceptual: the more specific legal applications appear in later chapters. The activity may be thought of as any one which has as by-product a negative effect on another party. It could be driving a car (and injuring someone else), industrial production which produces pollution, listening to pop music in a public place, smoking, etc. It is presumed that there is a social interest to be served by resolving the conflict of interest which exists between the parties. For present purposes this social interest may be served by the legal system through the courts.

Note that granting or not granting an injunction simultaneously determines the entitlement and how it is to be protected. The protection is absolute, it cannot be infringed. However, it can be transferred with the entitlement holder's consent, i.e. the entitlement holder can agree not to seek an injunction or having had one granted may agree to request its dissolution. This has been identified by Calabresi and Melamed as a *property rule*. They have suggested, however, that this is not the only possibility. They suggest that an alternative approach is to use *liability rules*.

The most obvious liability rule is one which imposes liability on the injurer for all 'unreasonable' damage. Liability (or damage) remedies are probably most readily associated with torts – in particular, unintentional torts such as accidents. However, interference with another's enjoyment of his property is conceptually the same to an economist as an accidental tort. What, in principle, is the difference between the two situations? Is it simply that one act is intentional and the other is not? An externality caused by the action of one individual may not be intentional in the sense that he did not set out to harm the other individual: it is *by-product* of an intentional act.

Looking at accidents (which fall within the confine of tort law) it is obvious that market transactions and the consequent voluntary exchange of entitlements is not possible. Each driver cannot negotiate with all potential accident victims for the exchange of the entitlement to be free from bodily injury, which is what would be involved in protecting victims by a property rule. Imagine that only a property rule were available to protect accident victims, i.e. that there was an absolute right to physical safety. A driver would then have to negotiate *in advance* with every potential accident victim to obtain a waiver of that right. Such negotiation would be prohibitively expensive and few people would drive. Society would lose the very great benefits which its members obtain from driving because of the potential costs which could be imposed on others. i.e. driving would not be Pareto Optimal.

Society has evolved another remedy to handle this situation. Victims are compensated *ex post* for any injury. Note that such compensation, however, is not *negotiated* between the parties but is *imposed* by the judgment of a court. Damages are 'socially' imposed.

In the case of accidents, *ex post* negotiation is almost as futile as *ex ante* negotiation. The accident has occured and the victim has every incentive to overestimate the acceptable compensation while the injurer has every incentive to underestimate it. Strategic behaviour raises its head once again.

The purpose here is not to discuss in detail accidental torts but to point out that the fundamental reason for the use of the damage remedy in such instances is that a negotiated solution is unlikely, and to point to the similarity between this situation and that of a conflict in property rights encumbered by strategic behaviour. Thus in a case, say, of a single polluter and many victims when 'free-rider' or 'hold out' problems might preclude the exchange of an entitlement through negotiation, the court could decide who should have the entitlement and, if appropriate, compensate for its infringement through the award of damages.

Consider a hypothetical situation in which an 'injurer' as a by-product of his activity imposes an external cost on 100 'victims'. The injurer makes a profit of £10,000 p.a. and each victim suffers an 'injury' for which £50 would be adequate compensation. Suppose that the injurer could avoid creating the injury by adapting this activity at an annual cost of £7500 and that each victim could protect him/herself by installing protection at a cost of £25 p.a. Table 5.1 illustrates the benefits (+) and the cost (–) to each party of permitting the injurer to operate under different conditions.

Table 5.1

	Injurer	Victim	Net Effect
(a) Injurer operates	+10000	–5000	+5000
(b) Injurer adapts	+2500	0	+2500
(c) Victims install protection	+10000	–2500	+7500

Clearly the optimum solution is to have the victims install protection. If there are zero transaction costs this could be achieved by giving either party the entitlement:

(i)   Grant an injunction to the victims who could be bought off by the factory buying each a protector.

(ii) Refusing an injunction would lead to each victim installing protection.

Now suppose transaction costs preclude bargained solutions because of hold-out and free-rider problems on the part of victims. A property rule giving the entitlement to the victims would not guarantee that the injurer could negotiate round it. The outcome would be that the injurer adapts his activity and net benefits of only £2500 p.a. would be attained. If the injunction were refused the victims would be forced to install protection and net benefits of £7500 p.a. would be attained. Consequently a court concerned solely with efficiency should refuse the injunction in this case. The reason for this is that the victims are the *lowest cost avoiders of the 'injury'*. Thus where a bargained solution is not possible a court should grant the entitlement to the higher cost avoider.

What if the court does not know who the lowest cost avoider is? This is quite common. In such a case the court does not have the information contained in rows (b) and (c) of the Table. Let us assume that it does have the information contained in row (a), i.e. it is possible to ascertain the benefits and costs of the parties. A court imbued with the Kaldor–Hicks notion of efficiency would grant the factory an entitlement to operate: 'The social utility of the ... activity outweighs the private costs.' Notice that this would be converted to the optimal solution in this particular case because the lowest cost avoider is *not* the party who values the entitlement most. Thus if the injurer could adapt the activity for less than £2500 p.a. but the court did not know this, the efficient solution could not be reached by giving the entitlement to the party who values it most.

An alternative would be to move away from a property rule to a liability rule. Thus the court, given the knowledge contained in line (a), could give the entitlement to the residents and subject the injurer to damages of £50 p.a. to each of the 100 households. Since the injurer's profits exceed £5000 p.a. if it produces, it will produce and pay the damages. Rational victims would then buy protectors and convert the outcome to (c), except that the profits of £7500 p.a. accrue £5000 to the injurer and £2500 to the victims. If the injurer did not value the activity at greater than £5000 p.a. it would cease production and efficiency would also obtain. Thus, even if the court were uncertain about the benefits but knew the costs, the damage remedy would still produce the efficient outcome.

The court could also employ another liability rule. It could give the entitlement to the injurer but allow the victims to buy it out at a judicially determined price equal to the foregone profits. This obviously requires a means of sharing that price amongst the victims. If this were possible the victims would only exercise their right if they valued the absence of injury at more than £10,000 p.a. and the efficient outcome would be obtained. Thus, it appears that in an uncertain world the damage remedy should be used; but it does not matter who is

given the entitlement, if efficiency is the only criterion.
So far, the analysis has been complicated by introducing transaction costs which preclude bargained solutions and uncertainty about who is the lowest cost avoider. Circumstances may arise where there is an asymmetry of transaction costs. It is conceivable that while the victims may not be able to organise themselves into a group to buy out the injurer's entitlement to carry out the activity there may be little likelihood of hold-out problems if the injurer has to buy out the victims. This would suggest that even in uncertain conditions the court should grant an injunction and allow the injurer to buy it off, i.e. the relative size of transaction costs might dictate which property rule should be chosen.

Similarly, the costs of arriving at the two liability solution may not be the same. The costs here are of valuation and coercing compliance. Thus it is possible that it will be easier to assess the loss of profits to the injurer than the loss of utility of the victims but it may also be easier to enforce the decision on the injurer than on numerous victims. (Short-cuts may also be achieved by using 'reasonable man' rules to assess the damage on individuals.)

The choice of entitlement holder and the means of protecting the entitlement may also be influenced by distributional considerations. If the victims in the numerical example were relatively poor, using the lowest cost avoider criterion, where a negotiated solution is not possible, might offend against distributional considerations. On the other hand, giving the victims the entitlement and protecting it by a property rule would sacrifice efficiency. Thus, we might wish to choose liability as a means of attaining both even when the cheapest avoider is known. A court could give an entitlement to the victims protected by a damage remedy. If the costs of adapting the activity were readily known damages might be assessed at only £25 p.a. per victim rather than £50 p.a. The former would protect the income of the victims and attain the efficient allocation of resources. The latter level of damages would attain an even greater redistribution. Clearly the latter could be justified on non-distributional grounds as compensating for the 'damage' but it is clearly not the minimum compensation. Thus the choice of the basis of assessing 'damage' may be influenced by distributional considerations.

If the victims were rich and the injurer a factory employing people with no alternative employment, or the factory's profits were £8000 p.a. and the victim's losses £10,000, then efficiency would dictate giving the entitlement to the victims but that would have adverse distributional consequences. Giving the entitlement to the injurer, but protecting it by a damage remedy, would give the victims the right to stop the injury. Damages would be assessed at £8000 p.a. which would allow the factory to adapt the activity and maintain employment, satisfying efficiency and equity.

The above examples implicitly suppose only two possible levels of the activity: zero, or that yielding £10,000 profit to the injurer. A more general formulation would be one under which the benefit to the injurer (profits, utility) rose but at a decreasing rate as the level of the activity increased. This would yield a downward sloping marginal social benefit curve for the activity similar to that depicted in Figure 4.4. The effect on the victims might be represented by an upward sloping marginal social cost curve (increasing disbenefit but at a decreasing rate) as in Figure 4.4. such a situation is depicted in Figure 5.1 where $A B$ is the marginal social benefit curve and OC the marginal social cost curve. It should be noted that activity level Q^* is efficient in a Kaldor–Hicks sense. The entitlement of the victims could be specified in terms of the level of the injurer's activity, or a level of damage, or a level of victims' well-being. However, since all of these are inter-related via the relationship of OC to the injurer's level of activity, which is used as the numeraire to specify the entitlement is immaterial, i.e. $\pi_v = \overline{\pi} - \delta(q)$

where π_v = the welfare of the victims

$\overline{\pi}$ = the welfare of the victims when the activity of the injurer is zero

$\delta(q)$ = the function relating the injury to the level of activity (q).

The injurer's entitlement could be specified as a level of activity or a level of benefit (or indeed a level of injury to the victims) but again these are uniquely related since

$\pi_1 = \pi(q)$

and $\delta = \delta(q)$

so that specifying a level of benefit implies a level of activity which in turn specifies a level of damage. In fact, specifying either party's entitlement specifies the other's and however the entitlement is described it can be thought of as specifying the injurer's output. Thus if a victim is given an entitlement to be free from damage it is equivalent to specifying zero output for the injurer. If it is specified as £x of damage it is equivalent to specifying the injurer's output to be q_E where the area of $\Delta ODq_E = x$.

If the entitlement point is to the left of q^* it is not efficient. Gains can be made from bargaining on how ΔDFE could be divided between the injurer and the victims, or some authority could direct the injurer to produce at q^* and redistribute the

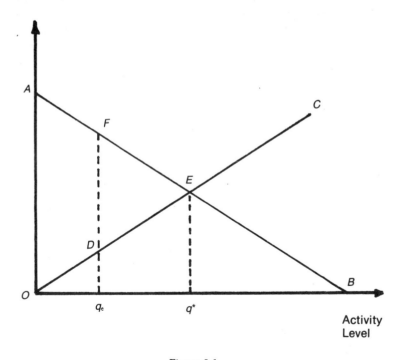

Figure 5.1

gains from moving from q_E to q^* so that injurer and victim were at least as well off as at q_E.

Indeed much economic analysis of externalities is conducted in terms of taxing the generator of the externality so that he produces the optimal output, q^*. There is, then, the distributional question of whether the victims should receive compensation to return them to their entitlement (or indeed improve upon it). Here, however, we are concerned with judicial means and, therefore, are precluded from consideration of direct government intervention. Note that the entitlement point can lie anywhere between O and B. (Beyond B is irrelevant since the injurer would not wish to produce more than OB.)

Having chosen the entitlement point the court must decide how to protect it: by a property rule or by a liability rule.

(i) *Property rule:* This entitles either party to block any move from the entitlement point. Say it is at q_E: the injurer will wish to move beyond q_E in order to capture as much of the benefits shown by $q_E FB$ as possible. To do so imposes injury represented by the area to the right of $q_E D$ and below OC on the victims who are entitled to resist such a move. The injurers could persuade the victims by compensating them for any damage but it would only be worthwhile doing so up to q^* because beyond that the necessary compensation exceeds the injurer's gain. Thus, essentially, the parties would be bargaining over the area $q_E FEq^*$.

The absence of strategic behaviour would mean that the victims would settle for a minimum of $q_E DEq^*$. Bargaining is essentially over the share-out of DFE which will depend on the relative abilities of the injurer and the victims as bargainers. However, stragetic behaviour many preclude q^* being reached and how any gains will be split is, in that case, indeterminate.

(ii) *Liability rules* remove each party's right to block moves from the entitlement and substitute in it splace and right to be compensated on a judicially determined basis when forced to move from the entitlement point.

Again, assuming q_E is to the left of q^*, a move to q^* is socially desirable. What an efficiency-minded court must do is design a damages schedule that will lead to output q^*. The most obvious one is where damages are equal to the value of actual injuries to the injured: i.e. the injurer must indemnify the victims for all damage caused in increasing output from q_E to q^*. Thus output is at the efficient level q^*, the injurer makes profits of $0AEq^*$ of which q_EDEq^* is transferred to the victims as compensation. The victims, therefore, suffer net damage of $0Dq_E$; and the net benefit to society is $0AE$. Note that the net benefit to society will always be $0AE$. What the different entitlements and liability rules do is specify how the gross benefits and costs are shared between the parties (the Coase theorem).

Liability schedules need not be identical to the marginal damage schedule: there could be over-compensation or under-compensation. All that is needed to get output q^* is that the damage schedule pass though E.

The choice of damage schedule may reflect a distributional choice to favour either the victim or the injurer. A number of points should be noted here:

(a)   if the marginal liability schedule lies above the actual marginal injury schedule strategic behaviour may rear its head because the injurer can deny surplus to the victims by refusing to increase output. Thus q^* may not be reached and the distribution of the net benefit is indeterminate. Therefore the position is similar to that under the property rule with the same entitlement point except that only a subset of the latter positions may be attainable. (The victim cannot do better than the liability schedule but he might as a superior bargainer under a property rule.)

(b)   If under-compensation takes place the injurer will choose to produce q^*. In the limit, victims could be reduced to just their position at q^* and the best that the injurer could get would be his profits at q^*. This of course corresponds to their position with the entitlement point at q^*. Thus the output and distributional outcomes with under-compensation could be attained by a property rule with a different choice of entitlement point.

(c)   If there is over-compensation and the marginal liability schedule corresponds to the injurer's marginal profit schedule, then all gains from trade would be subject to extortion and we would be back to the same set of outcomes as under the property rule.

(d) If q_E is greater than $q*$ the roles are reversed.

What all this leads to is that the choice between a property rule and liability rule depends on the technology of the externality (i.e. the relationship between the injurer's output and the victim's utility), the distributional preferences of society and the bargaining behaviour of the parties. It is therefore a complex choice which is not independent of the particular circumstances of a case. The options of a property rule or a liability rule provide a flexible means of obtaining society's desired goals (Polinsky, 1979; 1980a; 1980b).

These two instruments for protecting entitlement together with the Kaldor–Hicks criterion developed in the preceding chapter provide a conceptual framework for the analysis of a range of legal problems. The present chapter has abstracted from the nature of the legal conflict in order to stress the generality of the approach to conflict resolution. This avoids the compartmentalisation of remedies which flows from the usual legal subdivision. The material in the remaining chapters is grouped, broadly, on the usual legal lines but the analysis uses the conceptual framework developed in this and earlier chapters.

This chapter has discussed at an abstract level how courts might deal with a dispute arising from the activities of one party and its effect on others. This is a two-stage process. First, the entitlement must be decided; secondly, a means of protecting the entitlement must be found. Two such rules have been identified: a property rule and a liability rule.

There is a natural inclination to see this in terms of how the plaintiff's entitlement may be defended. But it may be the defendant who wins the case and therefore his entitlement has to be defended. Thus there are in principle four possible outcomes as summarised in Table 5.1

The first two of these are quite straightforward. The court finds in favour of the plaintiff and (i) awards an injunction restraining the defendant from continuing the offending activity, or (ii) awards damages against the defendant. This latter can be seen as a judicially imposed bargain between plaintiff and de-

Table 5.2

		Remedy	
		Injunction	Damages
Entitlement	Plaintiff	(i)	(ii)
	Defendant	(iii)	(iv)

fendant: in the case of damage already done the transaction cost are infinite and therefore a voluntary bargain is out of the question. In the case of damage to be done in the future it is really like a compulsory purchase of the plaintiff's right to be free to the offending activity. If the court finds for the defendant (iii) is formally equivalent to granting him an injunction restraining the plaintiff from restricting him in the exercise of his entitlement. Cell (iv) of the matrix seems to be the least plausible: the court finds for the defendant and awards damages *in favour* of him! But in terms of our analogy with a judicially imposed bargain it may make sense: it is the compulsory purchase of the defendant's right to undertake the activity.

These four options are logically available to courts. The law-and-economics literature would suggest that the pursuit of efficiency would dictate which the courts should (or would) choose. But do the courts perceive themselves as having these options. What do courts do? In subsequent chapters the doctrines adopted by courts to deal with different types of conflict will be analysed using, *inter alia*, this framework.

6 Property

This chapter is concerned with the economic analysis of the law relating to property. Such a treatment cannot hope to be comprehensive in a book of this length, therefore three areas of the law relating to property have been selected. These are (i) nuisance, (ii) the public regulation of land use, and (iii) the public acquisition of land other than by a market transaction. The first is the common law's means of resolving conflicts involving an interference with a property owner's right of enjoyment of this property. It frequently involves conflicts between adjacent landowners. The second topic introduces the statutory regulation of land use which in many jurisdictions have been introduced as a means of avoiding land-use conflicts previously dealt with by the common law of nuisance. Such regulation alter the rights of property-owners and may so limit such rights as to be tantamount to a 'taking' of the property. Most jurisdictions make provision for the property-owner to be able to obtain compensation for such a taking. Public authorities may also be empowered by statute to acquire land from its owner without the latter's consent using a statutory procedure. These two aspects of relations between property-owners and the state are the subject-matter of the third section of this chapter.

NUISANCE

Sturges v. *Bridgman* ([1979] 11 ChD 852) may be seen as a paradigm case of the law of nuisance: the lawful exercise of his property rights by one individual (confectioner) interfering with the enjoyment of another (doctor) of his property rights: a conflicting exercise of property rights. In economic parlance one activity has an external effect on another. The law of nuisance is the means by which common law courts seek to resolve such disputes. The law of nuisance by and large looks to the plaintiff's (pursuer's) interest: it seeks to protect the property holder's interest. It may be used as protection against smells, noise, invasion of privacy, nervous shock, enjoyment of recreation, loss of business due to noise or dust, etc. These rights, however, are not always absolute but are often protected against *unreasonable* interference. What might be a nuisance if it persisted over a long time period may not be if it is of short duration, e.g. temporary building works. What is reasonable in one locality might be unreasonable in another. To quote the judge in *Sturges* v. *Bridgman*: 'What would be a nuisance in Belgrave Square would not necessarily be so in Bermondsey.'

The law of nuisance, as it has developed in England and the United States will be examined using analytical concepts introduced earlier in this book.

England
Stephen Tromans (1982) points out that although English courts behave as though an injunction is an obligatory remedy in nuisance cases, it is in fact discretionary in terms of the Rules of the Supreme Court and Lord Cairn's Act of 1858 (now replaced by The Supreme Court Act 1981).

The basic position may be summed up under two principles. The first stating the primacy of injunctive relief is in the judgment of *Pride of Derby* v. *British Celenese* ([1953] Ch 149, 181).

If A proves that his proprietory rights are being wrongfully interfered with by B, and B intends to continue the wrong, then A is prima facie entitled to an injunction, or he will be deprived of that remedy only if special cirumstances exist.

In *Shelfer* v. *City of London Electric Lighting Co.* ([1895] Ch 287, 322), the principles outlining when the damages alternative should be used were stated thus:

(1) If the injury to the plaintiff's legal right is small
(2) or is one which is capable of being estimated in money
(3) or is one which can be adequately compensated by a small money payment
(4) or the case is one in which it would be oppressive to the defendant to grant an injunction.

As Anthony Ogus and Genevra Richardson (1977) point out, this suggests that only in cases where the defendant is the cheapest cost abater or the best briber should the injunction be preferred. Tromans points out further that three of the four conditions are concerned with the plaintiff's rights and only one with the defendant's. Wider considerations are ignored.

There is little concern – at least in the early cases – with the weighting of the costs and benefits (a la Kaldor–Hicks). See for example *Pennington* v. *Brinsop Hall Coal Company* ([1877] 5 Ch. D769), where the plaintiff complained of pollution of a brook which resulted in his cotton mill boilers becoming corroded. Closing the mill was estimated as a loss of £190,000 and 500 jobs, while the injury amounted to, at the most £100 per year. This defence was rejected and a perpetual injunction granted. In terms of the Coase theorem it would be interesting to find if the Coal Company bought out the injunction. Similarly, the case of *AG* v. *Birmingham corporation* ([1858] 4 K & J 528) demonstrates an unwillingness to balance the public interest against a private loss. Here the riparian owners of the River Tame sought an injunction against the Corporation (city authorities) for the pollution of the river with the city's sewage. Counsel for the Corporation argued:

... if the court should interfere ... the entire sewage of the town will overflow. Birmingham will be converted into one vast cesspit, which in the course of nature, from the great elevation of the town ... must empty itself into the Tame as before only in a far more aggravated manner. The deluge of filth will cause a plague, which, cannot be confined to the 25,000 inhabitants of Birmingham but will spread over the entire valley and become a national calamity.

The Vice-Chancellor interjected, 'We cannot talk of that in Court', and the injunction was granted.

Tromans argues that the courts are sometimes aware of the problems that this sort of approach might cause and have mitigated the effects in a number of cases by suspending the injunction temporarily or by qualifying the injunction to apply only at certain times. The position in England seemed to change somewhat with *Miller* v. *Jackson* ([1977] 3 All ER 338). Here the plaintiffs sought an injunction against cricket balls from the adjacent cricket ground entering their garden and damaging their property. The judgment of Lord Denning MR is a classic example of his style. The opening paragraph reads:

In summertime cricket is the delight of everyone. Nearly every village has its own cricket field where the young men play and the old men watch. In the village of Lintz in County Durham they have their own ground, where they have played there last 70 years. They tend it well. The wicket area is well rolled and mown. The outfield is kept short. It has a good club house for players and seats for the onlookers. The village team play there on Saturdays and Sundays. They belong to a league, competing with the neighbouring villages. On other evenings after work they practise while the light lasts. Yet now after these 70 years a judge of the High Court has ordered that they must not play there any more. He has issued an injunction to stop them. He has done it at the instance of a newcomer who is no lover of cricket. This newcomer has built, or has had built for him, a house on the edge of the cricket ground which four years ago was a field where cattle grazed. The animals did not mind the cricket. But now this adjoining field has been turned into a housing estate. The newcomer bought one of the houses on the edge of the cricket ground. No doubt the open space was a selling point. Now he complains that when a batsman hits a six the ball has been known to land in his garden or on or near his house. His wife has got so upset about it that they always go out at weekends. They do not go into the garden when cricket is being played. And the judge, much against his will, has felt that he must order the cricket to be stopped: with the consequences I suppose, that the Lintz Cricket Club will disappear. The cricket ground will be turned to some other use. I expect for more houses or a factory. The young men will turn to other things instead of cricket. The whole village will be much the poorer. And all this because of a newcomer who has just bought a house there next to the cricket ground.

His Lordship went on to distinguish the case from *Sturges* v. *Bridgman* arguing that under nineteenth-century law the right of the property-owner was in the ascendant.

But nowadays it is a matter of balancing the conflicting interests of the two neighbours. ... This case is new. It should be approached on principles applicable to modern conditions. There is a contest here between the interest of the public at large; and the interest of a private individual. As between their conflicting interests, I am of the opinion that the public interest should prevail over the private interest.

Lord Denning went on to suggest that he was inclined not only to refuse the injunction but to refuse damages in lieu of the injunction and in respect of past damages but since the cricket club did not oppose the award of damages he awarded £400 to cover all past and future damages. The appeal against the decision of the lower court was allowed. Ogus and Richardson saw this case as breaking new ground but Tromans argues that subsequent cases (though he only discusses two) have reverted to the traditional position. Tromans argues in fact that a consequence of the courts seeing an injunction as the only appropriate remedy has led to situations where the case has gone against the plaintiff because granting an injunction would be an exceedingly harsh judgment in the light of the damage that it would inflict upon the defendant (and possibly society at large). Tromans cites a number of cases.

One should be careful in reading Tromans' paper. He seems to be saying that the weight of the economic literature is behind the use of the liability rule. This is not so. The normative law-and-economics literature argues that judicial decisions should promote wealth-maximisation. The Coase theorem, of course, suggests that in the absence of transaction costs, bargaining will produce wealth-maximisation. However where there are significant transaction costs rules should be chosen that will lead to the wealth-maximising use being made of resources. As Calabresi and Melamed argue, where the cheapest cost avoider is known to be the defendant the injunctive remedy is appropriate even in the face of heavy transactions costs.

In the English cases discussed by Tromans transaction costs would not seem to be a major problem and therefore the injunctive remedy is appropriate. Indeed the one case where they might have been a problem is *Miller* v. *Jackson*. A reading of the judgments in the case seems to suggest that Mrs Miller had become unreasonable about the cricket field and that rational negotiation was out of the question. Hence the use of a liability rule. Lord Denning could certainly be read as arguing that the benefits of continuing cricket outweigh the losses. Note also that distributional considerations may be important. Where the plaintiff is an individual the nuisance may often have a non-pecuniary dimension which is difficult to assess. Where transactions cost are low bargaining may be a reasonable way to arrive at a valuation of the necessary compensation which will always err on the side of the plaintiff, thus distributing income towards him. In *Miller* v. *Jackson* a bargained solution was out of the question and the court felt that the public interest outweighed any measurement error.

It cannot, therefore, be concluded, as Tromans does, that English judicial practice is contrary to the law-and-economics literature. It can just as readily be argued that it is consistent with it. However this is, of course, no *proof* that the underlying logic is that of the law-and-economics literature.

The United States
If we turn to the United States there seems to be a different doctrine emerging which has been described as a 'balancing of conveniences' (*Spur Ind Inc* v. *Del E. Webb Developments Co* 108 Ariz 178 [1972]). The emerging doctrine appears to be in line with the economic analysis – at least in so far as it suggests the use of damages as an appropriate remedy.

The leading case in the US is now *Boomer* v. *Atlantic Cement Co*. (26 NY 2d 219; 257 NE 2d 870 [1970]9). This case concerned a large cement plant against which a number of neighbouring landowners brought actions for injunction and damages complaining of injury to their property caused by dirt, smoke and vibrations. Whilst the court underlined that its function was limited to settling the controversy of fairness between private litigants and not to promote the resolution of conflict public objectives, it weighed the loss suffered by the plaintiffs against the cost of removal of the nuisance. It pointed out that the loss suffered by the plaintiffs was the economic loss of the value of their property and that the defendant had invested over \$45 million in the plant and employed 300 people. Permanent damages were awarded.

It should be noted that in a dissenting judgment it is pointed out that permanent damages removed any incentive to alleviate the harm. However, in the main judgment it was argued that there was no prospect of alleviation. The *Boomer* judgment seems to have been followed in most US states. A very interesting US case is that of *Spur Industries Inc* v. *Del E. Webb Dev Co.* Spur Industries operated a cattle-feeding business in Maricopa County, Arizona, in a predominantly agricultural location. The business expanded from 35 acres to 114 acres by 1962, and by 1967 they were feeding between 20,000 and 30,000 head of cattle and producing about one million lb of wet manure per day. This produced a great deal of odour and flies.

In 1959 Del Webb began to purchase farmland some distance north of the Spur site to develop an urban area for retirement homes to be known as Sun City. The first development in 1960 was 2½ miles from Spur. But by December 1967 Del Webb's development had expanded to be within 500 yards of Spur. Del Webb then filed a complaint against Spur alleging that 1300 plots were unsuitable for sale because of the operation of the feed lot. The court concluded that Spur was a nuisance but since Del Webb had, in effect, come to the nuisance they should pay Spur the reasonable costs of moving or shutting down. In effect the nuisance should be bought out at a judicially determined price (cell (iv) of Table 5.1). The judgment was handed down at about the same time that Calabresi and Melamed published their paper indicating that such an option did in principle exist.

Most commentators seem to view the US courts as being much more flexible in their choice of remedy than the English courts. This is reflected in the former's greater willingness to award damages as the means of protecting entitlements.

There are a number of limitations on the use of nuisance law as a means of controlling harmful externalities. It is of course essentially a private remedy based on a property relation. The plaintiff must have a recognised property interest to have standing in a nuisance case. This excludes a perhaps large number of passers-by who may suffer because of the externality. Similarly if the loss suffered by such individuals (as well as those with a property interest) is individually small it may not be recognised by a court, even where in aggregate the loss is great. The recognition of public nuisance might be thought of as a solution here. A public nuisance is an interference with a class of individuals in their exercise of a right. However the treatment of public nuisance cases by the courts in both countries suggests its use to control externalities is limited (transaction costs).

Another limitation of nuisance law in controlling externalities arises from the existence of transaction costs: whilst the aggregate damage caused by the externality may exceed the benefits arising from the externality-producing activity (and therefore the Kaldor–Hicks criterion would suggest that stopping the activity increases welfare) the individuals adversely affected may not take any action because the costs of an individual action outweigh the individual benefits. Thus there is a potential 'free-rider' problem: a collectively rational suit is not individually rational.

Other Common Law Instruments
Jack Knetsch (1983, Ch. 10) has argued that the case-by-case approach which a nuisance law predicated on the law-and-economics literature's analysis of conflicts in land use involes has a major drawback: it increases the uncertainty surrounding investment in land. The security of an investment is reduced by the investor not knowing how a court might react at some time in the future when an (as yet) unknown use of adjacent land might claim nuisance. A doctrine based on wealth-maximisation would be likely to produce inconsistency across cases in that in some cases the entitlement would be found to lie with the noxious pre-existing user whilst in others with the incoming plaintiff. He argues that a rational, market-based approach would be to require noxious users of land to purchase easements from surrounding landowners, thus internalising their externality. The surrounding landowners would be compensated for the loss in the value of their land and potential purchasers of the surrounding land for a use requiring the cessation of the noxious activity would require to 'buy back' the easement. Entitlements would be clear and certain. Circumstances might still arise where the owners of an easement held out against a purchase of the easement which would unambiguously be in the interests of society. Knetsch

suggests that this possibility should be dealt with by some mechanism for the compulsory purchase of the easement. The issue however would still be fairly sharp: the value of the easement. Such a set of arrangements would have the virtues of certainty, consistency and efficiency.

Another private mechanism which has been canvassed as a means of controlling externalities is the restrictive *covenant* (see, for example, Ellickson, 1973). A party sensitive to a use (or potential use) to which a neighbour might put his land could purchase from the second party the latter's right do to what would otherwise be lawful: e.g. if *A* wishes to protect his attractive view he could pay *B* to refrain from building on the land in a manner which would block out the desirable view. Such an agreement would then be registered as a restriction on the use of land. Restrictive covenants are often used by landowners when they sell land to restrict the use to which it might be put or to regulate the aesthetic appearance of the development, e.g. many tenement buildings in Glasgow built in the late nineteenth century have covenants restricting the use of the properties to single family homes and the only permitted non-residential use is for medical practice; many modern housing developments in the UK are subject to covenants imposed by the developer restricting the height of hedges in front gardens; in the United States home owner associations have been formed to provide a means of restricting and controlling sub-divisions through the use of covenants (see, for example, Ellickson and Tarlock, 1981). It may be argued that the Coase theorem suggests that such a mechanism would generate the most efficient use of land since the covenantee must value the restriction more than the covenantor values its absence, otherwise a bargain could not be struck.

Any landowner seeking a restrictive covenant is likely to wish that it 'run with the land', i.e. be binding on the subsequent owners of the land. Clearly this makes the covenant more valuable to its beneficiaries (e.g. the party whose view is preserved). If it 'runs with the land' the covenant is more than a contract between the two original parties it is a land use restriction. Covenants are a problematic area of the law. In English law (though it would seem not in American or Scots law) only restrictive covenants can 'run with the land', i.e. a covenant requiring some affirmative action cannot be enforced. A further complication is that restrictive covenants must 'touch and concern' the land, i.e. must relate to the land and not some other aspect of behaviour such as that the owner must join a certain political party or provide manual labour, etc. Another complication is 'privity or estate'. For a fuller discussion of these see Ellickson and Tarlock (1981). One potential problem with restrictive covenants is their inflexibility: they shackle succeeding generations. A covenant valued at the time when it was struck may not be valued (or reasonable) many years later. However the courts (and in the UK the Land Tribunal) have shown themselves willing to terminate an outdated covenant.

Opponents of zoning in the United States (see further the next section) have argued that restrictive covenants provide a private alternative to public regulation (see Ellickson, 1973) and point to the example of Houston, Texas where there is no zoning (see Siegan, 1972; Fischel, 1985). The evidence from this single example is extremely difficult to evaluate. Undoubtedly private restrictions such as covenants raise transaction costs. The next section of this chapter looks at public regulation of land use by which the transaction costs associated with common law mechanisms might be reduced.

PUBLIC REGULATION OF LAND USE

The previous section of this chapter dealt principally with the law of nuisance. This was seen as the principle common law remedy for dealing with conflicts between landowners which arise from incompatible uses. The law of nuisance is reactive: the conflict of uses has already arisen. The other private remedies discussed above are somewhat more proactive: they are designed to stop a conflict arising. It has been argued that high transaction costs may restrict the use of both sets of common law remedies. An alternative which may give rise to fewer transaction costs is the regulation of land use by some public authority. Some schemes exist in all parts of the common law world. This section presents a model for analysing such systems. It is then applied to the system of zoning and subdivision control operated in the United States and the Canadian Province of Ontario, and development control operated in Great Britain. The model is an application of the property rule/liability rule framework outlined in the previous chapter.

A Model of Land-Use Regulation

Although there are differences in detail between zoning (supplemented with subdivision control) and development control, in operation they amount to the same thing: an attenuation of the entitlements of property-owners. Here we outline a general model which is then applied to land-use system, below. The approach has been used independently by Fischel (1985) in a US context, and by Stephen (1987) in British and Canadian contexts.

Land-use regulation of the type discussed below operates through a requirement that any development involving physical operations on land, a material change in land use or the intensity of land use obtain prior permission from 'some duly authorised body. One of the main purposes of such a regime is to prevent the development of incompatible uses. In other words, the system is a form of public regulation designed to prevent the generation of externalities in land use. It is usual for economists to distinguish between technological and pecuniary externalities. Only the former are relevant to questions of allocative efficiency; the latter represent a redistribution of economic rents. However, when the arguments of the social welfare function include questions of distribution as well as efficiency (as they surely do in the real world) both pecuniary and technological externalities are relevant to public policy-making. In the discussion below no distinction is made between technological and pecuniary externalities. Since externalities arising from land use are in the main localised in nature, the authorised body involved is usually an organ of 'local government'. For simplicity we shall call this body the *local planning authority* (LPA).

The LPA being part of local government machinery is likely to be responsive (or at least sensitive) to the interests of residents (being electors) within the geographical boundaries of its jurisdiction. It is therefore assumed that the LPA sees one of its primary objectives as the safeguarding of local residents' interests in the event of a proposal for a new development. This will be done be setting the minimally acceptable specification for the proposed development. In many political systems local government is not wholly autonomous. Its powers usually derive from legislation enacted by a superior tier of government. Given that such a superior tier of government will have a different constituency its objectives with respect to land-use controls will differ from those of the LPA. In what follows this higher tier will be referred to as the 'central government' (although in a federal system it may be the provincial and state government) and it is assumed that it is concerned with the allocative and distributional consequences of projects. Decisions of the LPAs will be subject to appeal to and review by 'central government' or a body appointed by it. (It should be noted that this provision does not apply to the United States.) However, because of the statutory basis of the system we model here, decisions of LPAs and central government will also be subject to review by the courts. It is assumed that the role of the courts is to interpret the statutes and constitutions and to apply administrative and constitutional law in defining the entitlements of developers, LPAs and central government and to protect them.

How would such a scheme of regulation handle the conflict of interests between a developer and local residents with respect to a proposed development of a parcel of land? To simplify the discussion we will assume that a range of forms of development exists and that these can be characterised on a scalar which we shall call the *specification of the project*. The specification desired by the developer will be that which maximises his profits from the development. A land-use conflict will arise between the developer and other residents (or taxpayers) within the LPA's jurisdiction if the profit-maximising specification imposes externalities on adjacent land users (technological externalities) or local taxpayers (pecuniary externalities).

It is assumed that such externalities are a decreasing function of the development's specification, i.e. it is possible for the LPA to specify adjustments to the project which decrease the external effects of the development. These adjustments may relate to the physical characteristics of the development, the manner in which it is developed or a means by which the fiscal consequences for local government may be mitigated by the developer. We assume that such increases in specification exist such that marginal changes in the specification of the project bring about successive reductions in the level of externality which it generates until a specification is reached under which there is zero externality. The LPA is therefore in a position to condition its approval of the development on a specification of its choice being adopted. The marginal benefit to society of each specification for the project will be the monetary value of the marginal reduction in externality it brings about. This is referred to here as the *marginal benefit of compliance* with a given specification. This is shown in Figure 6.1 as a montonically decreasing function of specification. The developer's profit-maximising specification is designated $S\pi$. The specification at which there is zero externality is designated S_E. Clearly any specification other than $S\pi$ reduces the developer's profits (otherwise $S\pi$ would not be the profit-maximising specification). In Figure 6.1 the marginal benefit of compliance is positive at S_E and further benefits to local residents and taxpayers are obtained at higher specifications.

These, of course, represent net gains to local residents and taxpayers from the development which may take the form of physical benefits (amenities, public facilities, etc.) and/or fiscal benefits (contributions to local authority net revenues). Such marginal benefits are assumed to be montonically decreasing in Figure 6.1 to ensure a unique equilibrium. A more realistic specification of the marginal benefit of compliance function which gives rise to the possibility of multiple equilibria is presented below. The social cost of increased specification (assuming the developer's revenue is invariant with specifications) is the reduction in the developer's profits. In Figure 6.1 this is illustrated by the monotonically increasing *marginal cost of compliance curve*.

Within the framework of this model the LPA will only sanction the development of the parcel of land if it meets specification S_E. This will be unacceptable to the developer who will appeal against the decision. (Appeal is assumed to be costless.) Before discussing how the central government deals with the appeal, the informational and other assumptions of the model must be addressed. Assume the 'best of all possible worlds' in which there are no transaction costs and the redistribution of income is costless. Under these assumptions there is not trade-off between efficiency and distributional equity. The government has perfect information and can choose the specification which is allocatively efficient and then satisfy its distributional objective by a costless redistribution of income. The efficient specification of the project will be that at which the marginal social benefit of compliance equals the marginal social cost of compliance and is designated S^* in Figure 6.1. At specification S^* the developer's profits are reduced below their maximum level by an amount equal to the area of $S\pi SE^*$ whilst the residents suffer an external effect equal to the area ECS_ES^*. At any specification above S^* the marginal cost of compliance exceeds the marginal benefit of compliance and therefore social welfare is reduced. A central government concerned with efficiency would therefore amend the LPA's specification from S_E to S^*. If central government was unconcerned with the distributional consequences of land development it would do nothing else. To the extent that the distributional impact on local residents and taxpayers or developers entered the government's social welfare function it would costlessly redistribute income towards the preferred party and away from the other. However central government is not the final arbiter on disputes of this nature: the courts have a role to play. (In the US context the central government plays no role and the developers appeal directly to the courts.)

If central government decides on specification S^* either the developer or the LPA or both might seek judicial review by the courts. Where the central government's distributional preferences favour one of the parties the likelihood of legal action by the other party is high. Following Calabresi and Melamed, we assume that the court resolves the dispute in two stages: in the first it must decide where the entitlement lies and in the second it must decide which form of remedy it should use to protect this entitlement. In principle, the courts may settle the entitlement at any specification. In practice, the entitlement

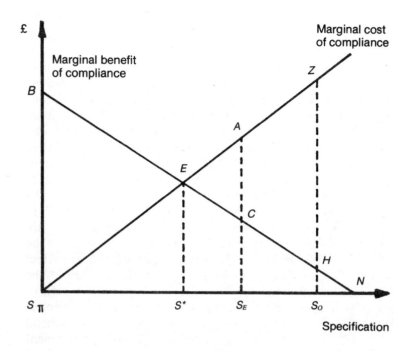

Figure 6.1

will be determined by the specific legislation involved, the court's interpretation of this, the court's view of its role *vis-à-vis* government interference with private property rights and other principles of administrative law. The analysis will be simplified by assuming that the courts take a black-and-white approach to this and settle the entitlement either in favour of the developer ($S\pi$) or the LPA (S_E). Selecting an intermediate entitlement does not radically change the analysis. The court may then protect the chosen entitlement by means of a property rule or a liability rule. A property rule in the present context would give either the developer the right to proceed with specification $S\pi$ or the LPA the right to impose specification $S\pi$. This need not be the end of the story because the parties may 'bargain around the injunction'. Thus if the court settles the entitlements at S_E the developer may try to bargain with the LPA for a lower specification in exchange for some form of compensation for local residents and taxpayers. Gains from such bargaining exist because at specifications above S^* the marginal cost of compliance exceeds the marginal benefit of compliance. Reducing the specification to S^* and having compensation equal to the area S^*ECS_E paid by the developer to local residents and taxpayers would leave the latter no worse off than at specification S_E whilst the developer is better off by the amount EAC. Such a bargain is possible in the 'best of all possible worlds'. The developer will not find it possible by such bargaining to attain specifications below S^* since at such specifications the required compensation exceeds the cost of compliance. Had the court settled the entitlement at $S\pi$ the LPA would have found it 'profitable' to compensate the developer for the cost of complying with any specification up to and including S^*. Thus regardless of where the entitlement is settled the use of a property rule and bargaining will achieve an efficient solution (assuming away the ask/offer problem discussed in Chapter 3 above). Costless redistribution could then be used to attain any distributional objectives.

A liability rule would be equivalent to the award of damages in the case of nuisance. If, for example, the entitlement lay at S_E the use of a liability rule would permit the developer to undertake the development at a lower specification subject to damage payments equal to the remaining level of externality. Since it is cheaper for the developer to comply with specifications below S^* than pay damages the developer would choose specification S^* and pay damages equal to S^*ECS_E. This would leave local residents and taxpayers no worse off than if specification S_E had been adopted but the developer would save EAC in potential costs. On the other hand if the court decided that the entitlement lay with the developer but the LPA set a specification greater than $S\pi$ the LPA would be required to pay damages equal to the cost of complying with the higher specification. The LPA would not enforce a specification above S^* since marginal damage payments would then exceed the marginal benefit attributable to the higher specification. Thus regardless of the point at which the entitlement is settled a liability rule would result in development taking place at S^*.

Under the assumptions of the 'best of all possible worlds' (perfect information, zero transaction costs and no strategic behaviour) the specification finally settled upon will be S^*, the efficient specification. Should this specification not accord with the government's distributional preferences the desired distribution can be attained (by assumption) via costless redistribution. Therefore, in the 'best of all possible worlds' the location of the initial entitlement and the means chosen by the courts to protect it do not alter the final outcome (i.e. the Coase theorem applies). However the real world is far from the 'best' of all possible worlds.

Earlier in this book it has been pointed out that transaction costs in the form of strategic bargaining and hold-outs militate against the use of a property rule since such behaviour may prevent a move from the initial entitlement to the efficient outcome being undertaken. Such analysis suggests the use of a liability rule which substitutes judicially assessed damages for the bargained compensation of the property rule. However it has also been argued that in a real world where information is asymmetrically distributed courts may not estimate damages correctly thus leaving further scope for bargaining among parties. The fact that redistribution of income is costly and that government may give a high weighting to distributional equity might not only determine to whom the initial entitlement be given but also how it might best be defended. In the present context the focus is on the existence of transaction costs arising from opportunistic behaviour. In particular, the LPA might behave opportunistically in arriving at the specification at which it will permit development to take place.

In Figure 6.1 S_O represents the specification at which the developer makes zero profits. Thus the area of triangle $S\pi ZS_O$ is equal to the maximum profits attainable by the developer. Specification S_E is that at which there are zero external effects. At specification S_E the developer still makes profits equal to the area $S_E AZS_O$. The LPA might behave opportunistically by setting the acceptable specification between S_E and S_O. Where the development is mobile competition between LPAs will militate against this. In such circumstances the developer will be able to play one LPA off against others thereby driving down the 'price' to be paid for development. Consequently, in the case of industrial development, an LPA might be willing to grant planning permission at a specification to the left of S_E because of compensating employment-generation by the project. On the other hand, many LPAs will have jurisdictions with unique features. Furthermore the larger the geographical jurisdiction of an LPA the more likely it will be for it to be have opportunistically. There is therefore scope for opportunistic LPAs to capture some of the economic rent represented by $S_E A Z S_O$. In a world of perfect information LPAs would not be able to act opportunistically since the court could easily identify S_E. In the real world courts will be sensitive to the possibility of such behaviour and look at the setting of entitlements carefully in this context.

Even where the entitlement is settled at S_E an opportunistic LPA may still seek to capture some of the developer's rents within the area EAC. If the LPA's entitlement is protected by a property rule it may attempt to extract compensation greater than $S^* E C S_E$ in exchange for reducing the specification to S^*. The LPA is in a relatively strong bargaining position since the developer requires permission to undertake the development: the alternative would be to develop without permission in the hope of damages being imposed in accordance with the marginal benefit of compliance schedule. However the developer would run the risk of being required to remove the development if the court stuck to a property rule. Thus the cards remain stacked in the LPA's favour. The developer's only option would be to behave strategically himself and refuse to develop. This would depend on the competitive position of the LPA *vis-à-vis* other LPAs. A property rule would only seem reasonable if public policy favoured a redistribution towards the LPA's constituents. Note also that if the LPA were behaving opportunistically the developer might be tempted to comply with specification S_E to 'spite' the LPA. Many writers in the nuisance literature have favoured a liability rule because of the pitfalls associated with strategic behaviour. In this context a liability rule might take the form not of post-development damages being awarded for failure to comply with specification S_E because this might be seen as risky for the developer but of *ex ante* judicially imposed compensation. Polinsky has argued that in conditions of uncertainty as to the true position of what has been called here the marginal benefit of compliance curve strategic behaviour may still be generated under a liability rule. However, in the present context, this might be overcome by requiring the LPA to make a detailed case for the level of compensation necessary to mitigate the external effects which would remain at the developer's proposed specification. The court would presumably require technical assistance in evaluating such a case.

The elaboration of the model thus far has assumed a monotonically declining marginal benefit of compliance curved as illustrated in Figure 6.1. A more realistic situation would be one in which the marginal benefit of compliance curve declined monotonically until it was zero at specification S_E, i.e. the specification at which the external costs of the development were zero. Specification greater than S_E would involve the generation of net benefits to local residents and taxpayers which might decline monotonically from some positive level. This is illustrated in Figure 6.2. BS_E is the marginal benefit of compliance curve for specifications up to that which removes the externality. FN is the marginal benefit of compliance curve for specification above S_E. The area of $S\pi BS_E$ is equal to the total external cost at specification $S\pi$. The area bordered by FS_E, FN and the horizontal axis up to any specification level below N represents the net benefits to local residents and taxpayers of any development taking place at a specification above S_E. If the marginal cost of compliance curve is $S\pi Z$ there is a unique social equilibrium at specification S^*. If however the marginal cost of compliance curve is $S\pi Y$ there are two specification, S' and S'', which meet the first-order condition for a social optimum (i.e. marginal cost of compliance = marginal benefit of complicance). S'' will be the social optimum if the area $GFE'' > S'E'S_E$. Thus 'opportunistic behaviour' on the part of the LPA may be socially optimal (at least within a partial equilibrium framework). On the basis of earlier arguments the courts will not be concerned with the social optimum but will settle on a specification at or to the left of S_E.

The Development Control System in Great Britain

The system of development control in Great Britain today

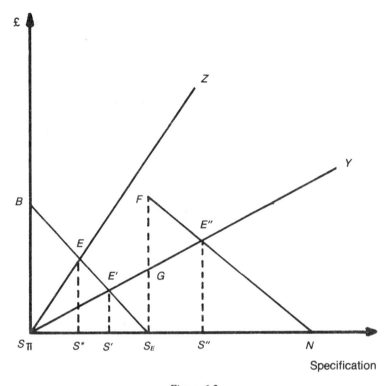

Figure 6.2

derives from the statutory schemes introduced by the Town and Country Planning Act 1947 and the Town and Country Planning (Scotland) Act 1947. These Acts have been amended on a number of occasions and the process is currently governed by the Town and Country Planning Act 1971 and the Town and Country Planning (Scotland) Act 1972. Although the system is governed by different legislation in England and Wales, and Scotland this largely reflects the different structures of local government. The overall framework is the same under both Acts. In what follows minor differences in the system will be suppressed.

Throughout Great Britain the general position is that any person who wishes to 'develop' land by carrying out any substantial physical operation or by making any significant change in the use of land or buildings must obtain planning permission from the local planning authority. If that authority refuses planning permission or imposes conditions which are not acceptable to the developer, an appeal lies to the appropriate minister. When planning permission is refused or granted subject to conditions it is only rarely that the applicant will be entitled to compensation (e.g. if the land is incapable of 'reasonably beneficial use'). Although changes of national government in the post-war period have led to differing proposed schemes for apportioning the development value of land between the developer and the community, the effect of planning legislation actually in force has been that the existing use, and the value of it, is the owner's but that there is no entitlement to develop the land through changing its use.

Although the local planning authority, which is an organ of local government, and the minister have a wide discretion as to whether or not to grant permission and as to the conditions (if any) to be imposed on a grant of permission, all statutory powers have legal limits; the courts refuse to countenance the notion of unfettered discretion. By means of the *ultra vires* doctrine the courts have exercised a significant degree of control over the discretionary powers of public authorities. The courts will declare unlawful an administrative decision which is not authorised by statute or which involves an 'abuse' of a statutory power in the sense that the power has been employed in a manner which, in the court's view, was not intended by Parliament.

Most abuses of statutory powers may be subsumed under the general heading of 'unreasonableness'. In the field of town and country planning statutory form is given to one of the principles encompassed in 'unreasonableness' by requiring the planning authority (and the minister on appeal) to have regard not only to the provisions of the development plan for the area, which sets out the authority's policies for the development and use of land in its area, but also to 'any other material considerations'. Decisions may be quashed by the courts if there has been a failure to consider a material consideration or if some irrelevant factor has been taken into account. This doctrine of relevant and irrelevant considerations has given rise to what has been described as 'incessant litigation'. The courts have little statutory guidance as to what are or are not material considerations other than that the statute relates to planning but that merely shifts the question to 'what is planning?'. In practice, whilst many decisions have been quashed for failure to take account of a material consideration, there have been very few occasions in which courts have said that a particular consideration is not relevant to planning (on this see further Stephen and Young, 1985). Nevertheless, as Underwood (1981) has argued, what is a relevant or material consideration is 'crucial ... for development control, and indeed for the whole town and country planning system, since it is through this concept that the limits to public intervention in the planning sphere are defined.'

Some commentators on the UK planning system have identified contradictions in the decisions of the courts and argue that the law is in state of confusion. Patrick McAuslan, in his book *The Ideologies of Planning Law*, sees this as arising from different ideologies at work in the courts and in town planning generally. The most important ideologies identified by McAuslan in the actions of the courts and governments are, first, the ideology of private property: that the law is mainly concerned to protect private property rights; and secondly, the public interest ideology: that the law should be used to advance the public interest, even against private property rights. This argument has been further developed in the work of Martin Loughlin whose views have been summarised by Underwood (1981) as follows:

... grounded in the ideology of private property, the courts have failed to recognise the qualitative change in the public/private relationship which has been introduced by the intervention of the planning system in the land and development market, i.e. the state contributes directly to the formation of private values by its restrictive 'zoning' of land on which potential values may be realised and by performing an essential role in providing basic physical infrastructure. Loughlin concludes that the 'social need' model of planning has been frustrated by the pervasive influence of market rationality in the administrative and legal structures of the planning system.

Similar comments have been made on the attitudes of the courts to the attaching of conditions to grants of planning permission. In terms of s.29(1) of the 1971 Act and s.26(1) of the Scottish Act planning authorities are empowered to grant planning permission 'subject to such conditions as they think fit'. Although this power seems to confer a fairly wide discretion on a local planning authority, its use has not gone unchallenged in the courts. Three tests of such conditions have been set out by the House of Lords in *Newbury District v. Secretary of State for the Environment* ([1981] AC (578)). The tests are (i) conditions must be for a planning purpose, (ii) conditions must be fairly and reasonably related to the permitted development, and (iii) conditions must not be unreasonable. The first two tests were outlined in an earlier case in which Lord Denning stated: '. . . conditions, to be valid, must fairly and reasonably relate to the permitted development. The planning authority are not at liberty to use their power for an ulterior object, however desirable that object may seem to them to be in the public interest.' This dictum has subsequently been approved by the House of Lords. Although these tests would not seem to impose a severe limitations on the discretion of planning authorities the courts have interpreted them fairly restrictively (see Deans, 1980; Grant, 1982; and Young and Rowan-Robinson, 1986). For example, the courts have quashed conditions restricting the type of housing that could be included in a development, in particular that a specified proportion of the houses in the development should be public housing. This might be reasonably seen to be a 'planning purpose', although commentators clearly differ on this. However, the decisions of the courts on this question would seem to be guided by the view that the local planning authority had an ulterior purpose in mind: that of shifting the burden (or part of it) of providing public housing from itself to a private individual. A similar argument applies in cases where it may be the local authority's obligations as the roads authority that are relevant and where the condition requires the developer to *dedicate* land for public use as playing areas and open space in a proposed residential development.

Concern of local planning authorities as to the implications of particular developments for their statutory obligations has already been mentioned with respect to roads and public housing. Similar but varying consideration apply to other statutory obligations of local authorities relating to social and physical infrastructure: in particular education and sewerage and drainage. Undoubtedly there are fiscal implications of development for such functions. Courts are concerned that local planning authorities may be using their discretionary powers to force developers to accept the financial burden of providing facilities which some public body has a statutory obligation to provide. In terms of the model of the preceding sub-section the courts are concerned to ensure that local authorities do not use their powers as planning authorities to capture developers' rents in order to reduce the fiscal burden of the local authority's other statutory obligations. This finds expression in the court's concern with the materiality of considerations and the tests which conditions must pass. These are all directed towards defining the entitlements of developers and local planning authorities.

Malcolm Grant (1982) has argued that the UK courts have wavered between a 'privilege' theory and a 'private property' theory of the power to impose conditions. The former holds that a planning permission is a privilege rather than an entitlement and that developers may be called upon to bear all the social costs occasioned by their development. However Grant argues that the overall trend has been to favour a 'private property' theory under which planning control is seen as an interference with established rights and that applicants are entitled to planning permission in the absence of cogent reasons to the contrary.

In terms of the model outlined above, having defined the LPA's entitlement the court must choose a means of defending that entitlement. The British courts in keeping with their approach in nuisance cases adopt a property rule. They do not impose a judicially determined planning decision on the parties. Where the planning authority has, in the court's view, behaved unreasonably or imposed a condition which fails its tests the matter is returned to the planning authority for further consideration. In particular the courts have seldom severed a condition which they have considered unlawful from a grant of planning permission. Quashing a condition of any significance usually means that the whole decision is quashed. The local planning authority's right to make the planning decision is not abrogated. Where their decision to grant permission subject to conditions is quashed, the planning authority might, for example, decide to refuse permission altogether. The court has settled where the entitlement lies. It is up to the parties (developer and planning authority) to bargain around that entitlement but the consent of the planning authority must be obtained before development can take place – the essence of a property rule. Furthermore, the UK legislation makes no provision for charges to be levied by the planning authority for the right to develop. A developer might, however, find himself liable to a charge imposed by the water authority for the cost of providing a trunk system via which the waste from the development could be disposed (the developer is responsible for all 'on-site' works necessitated by the development). There is therefore only a limited statutory framework within which negotiations between the planning authority and a developer can take place. Such negotiations may be seen as a prelude to an acceptable proposal for development being submitted to the local planning authority. It is doubtful whether any 'side payments' from the developer to the planning authority could be enforced as part of a planning decision. It is to be noted that a planning permission runs with the land and is therefore not limited to the person who makes the application. The planning authority could not impose an agreement by the original applicant to make some form of side payment (monetary or 'in kind') on a subsequent owner of the land as part of a planning decision.

Notwithstanding these comments on the limited role within the British system for bargaining around the planning authority's entitlement there is one provision of the Town and Country Planning Acts which permits bargaining outwith the scrutiny of judicial review: planning by agreement. Section 50 of the Scottish Act provides that a local planning authority may enter into an agreement with a developer 'for the purpose of restricting or regulating the development or use of land, either permanently or during such period as may be prescribed by the agreement' (s.50; cf. s.52 of the English Act). Such agreements, if they are appropriately recorded, are enforceable at the instance of the planning authority against any subsequent owner of the land. The principal advantage to be gained by the local authority through planning by agreement is that it permits the local authority to obtain material benefits or control aspects of development which if attempted by attaching conditions to a grant of planning permission would be *ultra vires.*

Planning by agreement gives rise to the controversial topic of 'planning gain'. Martin Loughlin (1981) has defined planning gain

as the achievement of a material benefit or advantage by the local authority, which may be *ultra vires* if achieved by imposing a condition on a grant of planning permission, but which is nevertheless provided by the developer, although not commercially advantageous, in the expectation that the planning application will, as result, receive more favourable treatment.

This definition emphasises 'material benefit' or advantage, whilst that offered by the Property Advisory Group in its report *Planning Gain* (HMSO, 1981), would include benefits or advantages that are non-material in nature such as those of a procedural nature or which enhance the certainty of a condition's enforceability. A number of commentators have suggested that this definition is over-inclusive and that what is commonly described as planning gain is encompassed by Loughlin's more limited definition. A frequently voiced criticism of planning gain is that it is tantamount to a selling of planning permission: a planning authority may permit a development at a specification below that which it would normally regard as acceptable in exchange for the developer providing some facility or amenity unconnected with the proposed development. It should, however, be noted that planning by agreement is used differently in different parts of Great Britain. A survey by Jeremy Rowan-Robison and Eric Young (1982) of the use of planning agreements in Scotland suggests that only a few were designed to obtain planning gain as defined by Loughlin. Most planning agreements in Scotland would seem to be concerned with questions of procedure, certainty and to some extent flexibility of conditions. On the other hand, in London planning agreements are much more widely used to obtain planning gain.

In the context of the present paper it is unnecessary to enter into the controversial question of the ethics of planning gain.

What is relevant is that planning by agreement should be seen as a necessary and integral part of a development control system in which entitlements are enforced by a property rule. Earlier it was argued that the courts in Great Britain protect the local planning authority's entitlement to control development by a property rule. Without planning agreements bargaining around the LPA's entitlement is severely limited and thus moves towards efficiency are inhibited.

Zoning and Subdivision Control in the United States
Zoning first began on a large scale with the passing of a New York City ordinance of 1916. This was followed in 1926 with the promulgation of the *Standard State Zoning Enabling Act* (SSZEA) by a committee convened by the US Secretary of Commerce. Finally the Supreme Court in *Village of Euclid* v. *Ambler Realty Co.* (272 US 365 [1926]) sustained the constitutionality of the principle of zoning.

Space does not permit a detailed examination of zoning here: for a detailed examination of the law-and-economics of zoning in the spirit of the analysis below see Fischel (1985) and references cited therein. Basically, zoning involves the division of a municipality into a number of use areas. In each the zoning ordinance controls size of buildings, size and shape of plots, positioning of buildings on plots and the use to which land and buildings may be put. Attention usually focuses on use. A typical zoning ordinance might divide the municipality into zones of single-family occupancy, multi-family occupancy (i.e. apartments), commerce, light industry and heavy industry. Much finer divisions are possible: the modern New York City ordinance has 66. The powers are derived from the state's power to set up local municipal governments. Most state statutes enabling zoning have been heavily influenced by the SSZEA.

The delineation of use zones does have some basis in the idea of externality. It segregates uses which might be thought to give rise to externalities, e.g. housing and heavy industry. It implicitly assumes that like uses do not impose externalities on each other.

Zoning can be *cumulative* or *non-cumulative*. The original zoning schemes were cumulative. These defined a hierarchy of zones with single-family housing at the top and heavy industry at the bottom. A zoning scheme is cumulative if it allows a higher ranked use to be located in a lower ranked zone. Thus a single-family house can be built in an area zoned for heavy industry but a factory cannot be built in a single-family zone. Most modern zoning ordinances are non-cumulative. They prohibit the mixing of use classes, thus avoiding the potential problem of the owner of a house in an industrial zone suing for nuisance. It has also been suggested that since industry gives rise to higher local taxes provision should be made for it (fiscal zoning). However the courts have been hostile to such fiscal zoning.

In principle the American system should increase certainty and reduce conflicts. All landowners in a given use zone are treated alike. Undeveloped land in a given zone is available for the specified use and developers know, in advance, the use to which it can be put. There is no need to seek permission. The original zoning ordinances could be seen as the basis for forward-looking plans. Nowadays it is widely recognised that plans cannot be static and need to adapt over time as the situation changes. Thus Ellickson and Tarlock (1981) argue that zoning maps become 'first offers' and there is considerable case-by-case negotiation. Flexibility introduces discretion into the system. Whilst zoning maps usually recognise existing use patterns, undeveloped land is frequently allocated to a 'holding' zone (which in effect allocates it to its existing use). Change of use may require a variance of the zoning map which frequently will require some concession to be made to the municipal authority. Similarly municipal authorities can be persuaded to amend zoning regulations. Devices such as planned-unit development (PUD) and transferable development rights (TDRs) further loosen the system.

It has to be recognised that rigid pre-ordained zoning systems limit the transferability of property from one use to another as preferences change. Such a system could therefore be a source of allocative inefficiency. It is an empirical question whether such inefficiency is outweighed by the reduction in inefficiencies which would arise in the absence of regulation (e.g. externalities). A flexible zoning system may reduce allocative inefficiency but it increases the discretion of local officials which may raise questions of accountability and 'equal protection'. The exercise of zoning powers is subject to oversight by the courts. Since the *Euclid* case of 1926 the US Supreme Court has been involved relatively little in questions of zoning. Fischel (1985) points to increased activity since 1974. In none of the cases he cites did the Supreme Court overturn the local government's decision. Most of the court activity on zoning has been left to state courts. This has led to considerable inter-state variation. For the most part, issues relating to zoning come under the headings of *due process, equal protection* and *takings*. These are of course pre-eminently constitutional questions. The courts would seem to interfere infrequently with the municipal authority's zoning decisions.

Somewhat more contentious is a municipality's power to exact payment from developers wishing to subdivide existing land for muliple use, e.g. single-family housing developments. By and large it has been held by courts that it is constitutional to compel a developer to contribute to the financing of any physical infrastructure (roads, sewers, parks, land for school, etc.) where the developer's project created the need. Ellickson and Tarlock (1981) cite the judgment of the Missouri Supreme Court in *Home Builders Association* v. *City of Kansas City* (555 SW 2d 832 [Mo 1977]) as being the mainstream position. This decision regarding a requirement to dedicate land for recreational purposes lays down the condition however that 'the burden cast upon the subdivider is *reasonably* attributable to his activity'. This clearly suggests a move away from a property rule: it is not a question for negotiation but relates to the impact of the development on local residents and tax-payers. This 'objective' calculation is the essence of a liability rule. However, it is not quite a liability rule since the entitlement remains with the municipality. As Fischel (1985) points out, it is more akin to the leasing of the entitlement but the price of the lease is subject to judicial determination.

Some US state courts however diverge from this view: see, for example, *West Park Avenue, Inc* v. *Township of Ocean* (48 NJ 122, 224 A2dl [1966]). Here the argument is that such facilities are normally financed via local property taxes. Thus the developer is being made to pay for something which residents of existing developments are not – other than through taxation. This would seem sensible in terms of horizontal equity (see further pp. 115–18).

Ontario

The Canadian Province of Ontario controls the use of land through a combination of zoning and development control. The discussion here is based on Makuch (1983). Zoning's power to prevent incompatible uses of land in a given area is supplemented by a system of site plan control which requires detailed plans to be submitted to municipalities prior to any development taking place. The Ontario Act provides for municipalities to designate areas as site plan control areas. Such areas may be part or all of the municipalities. Detailed plans must be submitted for all developments taking place within such an area showing the location of all facilities and works. Development may not take place until such plans have been approved. The municipality has the power to require the owner to widen highways abutting the land and provide for access to and from the land, off-street parking and loading, walkways and pedestrian access, lighting, landscaping, waste storage, easements for water and sewerage, and grading. The plans and these other items can be made the subject of an agreement between the municipality and the developer which on registration will be binding on subsequent owners. The Act also provides for the dedication of parkland or payment in lieu of such dedication. However, these provisions cannot be used to control the height or density of developments. A system of density bonuses may, however, be provided in the official plan.

Further municipal control of land development is implemented primarily in suburban areas through the process of subdivision control which is used for land that is to be divided from large lots to smaller ones. Thus the creation of a new interest in land can be a focus for land-use controls. There is no obligation to approve a subdivision plan. Conditions can be attached to approval or require that the developer enter into agreements respecting the subdivision. The exercise of these powers is limited by their statutory provision and by providing for an appeal to the Ontario Municipal Board. The Lieutenant Governor in Council (provincial government) can intervene with respect to matters of provincial interest. Formally, sub-division control is a function of the Provincial Minister of Housing. Subdivision plans are circulated to Provincial Ministries and municipal and regional councils. The subdivision plan must conform to the official plan and to adjacent plans. Subdivision must not be 'premature' and must be 'necessary to the public interest'. Various physical factors must be considered, as must the adequacy of school sites, and the minister must have regard generally to the 'health; safety; convenience and welfare of the future inhabitants' (see Hudec, 1980). The Ontario Act also empowers the minister to require the developer to enter into an agreement with the relevant municipality with regard to the provision of municipal services and other such matters as the minister may consider necessary. Such agreements may provide for the imposition of a financial exaction on the developer. In practice, these matters have been dealt with by means of a standard condition such as

That the owner agrees in writing to satisfy all the requirements, financial and otherwise of the [municipality having jurisdiction with regard to the plan] concerning the provision of roads, installation of services and drainage. (Cited in Bucknall, 1981)

The municipal practice according to Bucknall is to agree that the municipality's standards with respect to land services within the project would be met and that the developer pay a levy usually calculated on a per lot basis, for the broad range of municipal services. In effect, then, the municipality has considerable discretion in setting conditions whether pec-uniary or otherwise on the development of land. In particular, the legislation lays down no basis on which such financial levies may be calculated. Some municipalities treat them as a matter for negotiation whilst others use standardised charges. In areas not subject to the site plan control procedure develop-ments may require a re-zoning of land which can give rise to a payment by the developer.

In terms of the model of land-use regulation outlined above, the municipality would seem to have an entitlement in deter-mining the conditions under which development may take place. During the 1970s the size of these financial levies grew rapidly and ceased to be related to the provision of specified municipal services. Often these were seen simply as a source of general municipal revenue. Hudec has argued that such levies can be justified on three grounds: (1) as user charges for the provision of municipal services, (2) as a method of internalising the costs of urban growth, and (3) as a method of redistributing the economic rents generated by the process of urban expansion. Our model of the development control process suggests that the last of these may be of some importance.

In fact, as the model of land-use control predicts, the courts have performed an important role in constraining municipalities' behaviour. The Ontario courts seem to be moving in the direction of a liability rule (cf. *Home Builders Association* cited p. 107 above). A benchmark case is one in which Lord Denning's dictum that conditions to be valid must 'fairly and reasonably relate to the permitted development' was quoted. This and subsequent cases (*re Mills and Land Divisions Committee of York* [1975] OR (2d)349) dealing with financial levies in the context of development conditions, dedication of parklands, condominium designations, re-zoning applications and land severance applications have shown that the courts and the Ontario Municipal Board do not regard municipalities as having an unqualified right to impose levies. Where the right to impose levies exists these bodies have required that the sums involved should be related directly to the development in question and be fair and equitable. In a number of these cases the levy imposed by the municipality was significantly reduced by the Ontario Municipal Board. In cases where a conversion to a condominium was involved and there was no evidence that the conversion itself imposed a fiscal burden the levy was struck down.

These decisions are not limited to the question of the muncipality's entitlement but deal with how that entitlement may be defended. They are consistent with the principle implicit in the mainstream position in the USA. The clearest statement of this is given by F.G. Blake, at the time Vice Chairman of the Ontario Municipal Board:

... in order to establish that the proposed special tax is reasonable or relevant ... a municipality at a hearing of this nature should provide evidence of the proposed municipal works for which the proposed levy is sought, their location, their estimated cost, the intended starting date of construction, the percentage of need caused by the existing population, and the amount of any fund already accumulated for works related to the severance. It would be difficult otherwise to make an objective decision with respect to the amount of the special levy that ought to be imposed.

As to the question of equity, Mr Blake also said:

The question of equity involves existing residential properties as well as new housing to avoid the possibility that special levies may subsidize existing residential properties. For example, if the need for a certain municipal works or park is caused equally by the existing population and the projected increase in population, a special levy should not be imposed at all because it would be an extra charge upon the new homeowner only in addiction to paying the same mill rates as an existing homeowner. (*Frey* v. *Phi Internat. Inc* [1977] 6 OMBR 444)

The latter reflects considerations of horizontal equity as outlined by Michelman (see below) and applied to suburban growth controls by Ellickson. Although Mr Blake's forthright statement has been softened in some subsequent decisions, the thrust of the Ontario system would now appear to be one of developers compensating municipalities for the external costs of a development rather than negotiations over financial terms under which the municipality is prepared to grant permission. The Ontario system as described here has a major feature which suggest that the Ontario Municipal Board and the courts are using a liability rule to defend the municipality's entitlement to control development: a judicially determined price at which the entitlement is transferred. However, it is not strictly a liability rule for that, as suggested earlier, would imply that the developer could act without permission but with a liability to *ex post* damages. The damages are however being determined *ex ante* in conjunction with a grant of permission. The Ontario system as operated does not abrogate the requirement for permission but regulates the terms associated with the grant of permission. It is neither wholly a property rule nor a liability rule but incorporates elements of both. Discussing the similar US position, Fischel (1985) has used the term 'leasing' of the municipalities' entitlement.

Conclusions on Land-Use Regulation

This section has considered the land-use controls in operation in Great Britain, the United States and the Canadian province of Ontario. While in all systems local government bodies have a considerable role in determining the nature of land-use development and the impact which a specific development might have on existing landowners and local taxpayers the courts have played a significant role in constraining this discretionary power.

These planning powers of local authorities have been shown to be a potential instrument by which existing residents might extract significant amounts of the development value of land from developers and redistribute it to existing residents and taxpayers (in the form of reduced tax bills or enhanced facilities).

It has been argued that British courts have exercised this constraint by a narrow interpretation of the planning body's entitlements whilst leaving undisturbed the means by which that entitlement might be defended. Thus the courts have implicitly employed a property rule which leaves the local authority in a position to dictate the terms on which development may take place. On the other land, the mainstream US position and that of the Ontario Municipal Board has constrained municipalities in their exercise of discretion by shifting to a mixed rule by which exactions in money or in kind must be related to the burdens imposed by the development. The model of development control outlined in the first subsection of this section suggests that such a system is less likely to involve a redistribution of development value than the British system. The evidence from the US and particularly Ontario suggests that the 'opportunistic' behaviour of planning bodies hypothesised by the model does exist. This may also be seen as vindication of the British courts' concern with the limits of local authority planning powers. However the model does suggest the means chosen by these courts to defend developers' rights may merely change the means by which local authorities extract these benefits. A change from imposed planning conditions to an imposed 'agreement'; although it must be recognised that both sides gain from the agreement. The Ontario Municipal Board has sought to determine the terms of such an agreement by making it compensatory in nature and subject to judicial review. Recently, however, the UK government has shown an increased interest in the terms of such agreements. Recent advice from the Scottish Development Department (SDD Circular 22/1984) and the Department of Environment (DOE Circular 22/1983) suggests that it is the appropriate ministers' view that the terms of such agreements should be such that developers are only required to make provisions which rectify any adverse effects of their development. This would seem to be a move towards the position taken by US courts and the Ontario Municipal Board. However this advice has not as yet been given the force of law by a judgment in the courts. Which system is to be preferred from a policy standpoint depends on the ultimate objectives of public policy: in particular whether the regulation of land use is to be a means of redistributing income from the owners of land with development potential to other members of the community. If this were an objective it might be better effected by an explicit legislative intent and definition of property rights than by *ad hoc* decisions and negotiations in 'smoke-filled' rooms.

COMPULSORY PURCHASE AND EMINENT DOMAIN

Most states have statutes which provide for the compulsory acquisition of private property by public bodies. There seems to be a general acceptance that circumstances will arise where the use of such powers is justified. Blackstone, in his *Commentaries on the Laws of England*, writes that such powers 'ensure that the good of the individual yields to that of the community'. Even the United States, that bastion of free enterprise and private property, provides for it. The Fifth Amendment to the United States Constitution limits such takings to those of 'public use' and requires that 'just compensation' be paid.

In the United Kingdom before 1845 such compulsory purchase was provided for by various specific Acts of Parliament which each specified the basis on which compensation would be paid. The Land Clauses Consolidation Act of 1845 provided a general code governing compulsory acquisitions which could be incorporated in any specific Act providing for such an acquisition. This Act became the authority from which the right to compensation derived (although only implicitly).

Much of what economists have to say on this topic relates to the basis on which compensation should be paid when land is to be compulsorily acquired. However, before getting into that question, let us begin by asking the prior question: Why should the state have the right to 'take' the land of an individual rather than acquire it on the market?

The Economic Argument for Compensation

Richard Posner in his book *Economic Analysis of the Law*, has argued that eminent domain (or compulsory purchase as it is called in the United Kingdom) is necessitated by the existence of monopoly power. Land, and particularly land in a given position, is unique. When a specific piece of land is required to complete a particular project, such as a road or railway track, the whole value of the project may hinge on acquiring that particular piece of land: the owner, in theory, could extract the whole of the projected benefit by refusing to sell the land at a lower price. Thus the price which he could extract could be vastly in excess of what could be obtained in any alternative use.

Posner further argues that this will increase the price of land relative to other factors of production used in building such right-of-way projects. This will lead, where possible, to a substitution of other factors for land. The opportunity cost of these other factors may exceed that of land and therefore allocative inefficiency will arise. This might lead us to suggest a Kaldor–Hicks-type justification for compulsory purchase: the gains from using the land for the road (or whatever) exceed the cost (in terms of lost output), therefore the transfer of the land to the building of the road is efficient. This would seem to suggest that expropriating the land without compensation is justified!

However, Posner is not arguing this. He argues that compensation is necessary to ensure that public authorities genuinely do value the land more highly than the owner. In a sense compulsory purchase is necessary because the market fails to operate competitively (indeed it arises from a sort of transaction cost). A judicially or statutorily imposed transaction is replacing a market transaction. Indeed this analogy with damages is enhanced by the formal steps required in a UK compulsory purchase which are similar to those of a voluntary sale except that compulsion is involved (see Davies, 1984, pp.24–7).

In addition to Posner's economic argument, most people might agree that the absence of compensation would be unfair – one citizen is required to 'pay' the cost of obtaining a benefit for the community. Some would argue that this is a distributional question and outwith the scope of economics (e.g. Kaldor) which is only concerned with efficiency. However this writer rejects this view since equity considerations do enter into economics.

Alternatively it could be argued that the requirement for compensation is justified in terms of the Pareto criterion, i.e. there should be no net losers. This writer would be reluctant to do so because of the inherently conservative nature of the Pareto criterion.

The Philosophical Argument for Just Compensation

Frank Michelman (1972) has explored in detail the philosophical underpinnings of compensation practices. He argues that underlying both a utilitarian (i.e. economic or efficiency) and a fairness (or justice) approach are the balance between efficiency gains and what he calls demoralisation and settlement costs. The *efficiency gains* (E) are essentially the net benefits as appraised by the Kaldor–Hicks criterion. *Demoralistion costs* (D) are the total of:

(i) the money value necessary to offset the disutility which accrues to losers and their sympathisers (or observers) from the realisation that no compensation is to be offered; and

(ii) the money value of lost future production by those who think that they may be the subject of such an uncompensated loss in the future.

Settlement costs (S) are the money value of resources required in order to reach a compensation settlement which would remove the demoralisation costs (not just in the instant case). Clearly if $E<S$ and $E<D$ the project should not be undertaken. If the project is to go ahead, clearly it is the lesser of S and D which is relevant: thus if $S<D$ (& $S<E$) compensation should be paid and if $D<S$(& $D<E$) compensation should *not* be paid.

Posner has argued that demoralisation costs are not relevant because so long as it were clearly known that compensation was not to be relied upon the risk of a taking would lower the price of property and no one would be demoralised, i.e. the price of property would fully reflect the right (or otherwise) to compensation should the property be taken. This, however, still leaves the problem of deciding which takings should be compensated and the demoralisation costs of introducing a no-compensation rule.

Michelman also argues that society's attitude towards compensation is influenced by whether the loss was occasioned by deliberate social action, for in these circumstances the individual runs the risk of losses being *systematically* imposed upon him. This of course could lead to an expending of effort and resource to ensure that one is not systematically imposed upon. Michelman then asks the question: 'What compensation practices will arise if they have the purpose of quieting people's unease about being systematically imposed upon?' Clearly compensation should be paid for capricious redistributions when settlement costs are low and where the victim has suffered an injury distinct from those suffered by the generality of people. Furthermore, 'practically' non-compensatable redistributions which have *arguable* efficiency gains should be subject to compensation. As the efficiency gains fall the case for compensation rises.

The need for a sense of security implicit in the utilitarian justification implies the need for additional information as to whether the burden is a rare or peculiar one, whether there is some reciprocity of burdens couple with benefits, or whether the class subject to the burden has extracted some compensation in 'kind'.

Michelman then turns to consider *fairness*. As a basis for this he adapts the work of the philosopher John Rawls. Rawls attempts to clarify the idea of justice as the special virtue of social arrangements within which inequalities in treatment become acceptable. Underlying Rawls' approach is the notion that social arrangements must be acceptable to all fully-informed, rational individuals acknowledging that they themselves might occupy the least favourable position. He finds that two fundamental principles would emerge:

(i) a general presumption that social arrangements would accord no preference to anyone (i.e. maximum liberty consistent with the liberty of others);

(ii) departures from (i) may be justified so long as everyone has a chance to attain the favoured position and that the arrangement can reasonably be supposed to work out to the advantage of every participant – especially the one who occupies the least favoured position.

Rawls' principles are then adapted by Michelman to be applied to the question of compensation. The analogue to Rawls' first principle would be a rule forbidding all efficiency-motivated undertakings which have the *prima facie* effect of impairing liberties unless compensating payments are employed to equalise impacts.

The second principle would justify the absence of compensation if it could be shown some other rule should be expected to work out best for each person in so far as his interests are affected by the social undertakings giving rise to occasions of compensation, i.e. when will a decision not to compensate be fair? Michelman argues that this hinges on the risks associated with the general practices respectively represented by a decision to compensate or not to compensate in this specific case. The risk associated with the more stringent requirement to compensate is that settlement costs will force the abandonment of efficient projects. The risk associated with the less stringent approach is that there will be concentrated losses from efficiency-motivated social projects which would otherwise not have been sustained.

A decision not to compensate is not unfair so long as the disappointed claimant ought to be able to appreciate how such decisions might fit into a consistent practice which holds forth a lesser long-run risk to people like him than if compensation was consistently given.

The relevant risks are minimised by an insistence on compensation when settlement costs are low, when efficiency gains are dubious, and when the harm concentrated on one individual is unusually great. They are minimised by not insisting on compensation when there are reciprocal benefits and burdens, burdens are imposed on many people (making settlement costs high and individual losses small).

Although the utilitarian and fairness approaches can diverge they will tend not to, where the publication of outcome is widespread and perceptive interpretation can be assumed.

The Basis for Compensation

Given that a 'taking' is justified, what should the basis of compensation be? In the United Kingdom and most Commonwealth countries it is statutory. In the United States constitutions, statutes and court decisions guarantee 'just compensation'. The Supreme Court in *Monogahela Navigation v. United States* (148 US 312 [1893]) expressed the view that compensation was for the property and not the owner. The current US and UK positions on 'just compensation' are similar, requiring compensation equal to the value which the property would obtain in the market on a free sale.

This has not always been the position in the UK. The Act of 1845, according to Widdicombe and Moore (1975), provided for two kinds of statutory compensation for interests acquired:

(a) the value to the owner of the land acquired, including compensation for the disturbance of his interest; and

(b) compensation for damage sustained by him in respect of other land held with the land acquired, by reason of severance or injurious affection.

The courts in implementing this right to compensation made the assumption that the value to be taken is that arrived at between an *unwilling* seller and a willing buyer. In a number of cases this resulted in sums of compensation that seem to reflect heavy damages. In general there was a tendency to add 10 per cent to the value of the property to reflect the fact that the transaction was compulsory.

What Widdicombe and Moore (1975) describe as the 'mischief of excessive compensation' was ended with the passing of the Acquistion of Land (Assessment of Compensation) Act 1919. The Act provided that 'no allowance shall be made on account of the acquisition being compulsory', and that the 'value of land shall be taken to be that amount which land if sold in the open market by a *willing* seller might be expected to realise'. It is not appropriate here to go into the details of the UK legislation. What is of significance is the uniformity of principle in the United Kingdom and the United States.

Before going on to consider whether the 'market value' test is the appropriate one, it will be useful to see where compulsory purchase fits into the law and economics scheme of things.

Earlier in this book the analogy of damages to a judicially imposed bargain was made. This idea carries over to the question of compulsory purchase: it may be thought of as a *statutorily* imposed bargain. In other respects, in the UK at least, the transaction goes through all the stages of a voluntary exchange.

It is perhaps useful to think of the situation as being one of very high transaction costs and therefore no voluntary bargain being possible because both sides have an incentive to behave strategically. Thus a property rule is not appropriate. We therefore have recourse to a liability rule: the award of damages for the state over-riding the owner's entitlement. The problem is in assessing damages.

The economic approach to assessing the appropriate level of damages is, perhaps, illuminating for non-economists because it is in conflict with their preconception of economics being financially-oriented or being the 'metric of the market'. Most economists would *not* accept that the market price is the appropriate measure of compensation!

What is needed is a measure of the loss of welfare to the owner of the acquired property. Is that represented by the market price? No! The market price is the value to the marginal consumer and in the case of 'reproducable' goods will be equal to the opportunity cost of the resources needed to produce it.

In discussing the concept of consumers' surplus in an earlier chapter it was seen that for a competitively supplied good all infra-marginal consumers value the good above its market price. Thus for them market price is not a true measure of value. In the case of many goods this would not pose too much of a problem. If the state were compulsorily to purchase your Mars Bar and compensate you with the price of a Mars Bar you could go out and buy another Mars Bar which yielded you an identical level of consumers' surplus. (To leave you totally indifferent you would have also to be compensated for the time and effort of replacing the Mars Bar.)

The Mars Bar case is pretty straightforward because one Mars Bar is a perfect substitute for any other Mars Bar but that is unlikely to be the case for real property (and house in particular). Each house will have specific characteristics (including locational ones) which cannot be replicated in another house – even one which sells for the same price.

Jack Knetsch (1983) makes this point graphically by suggesting that market value compensation is equivalent to saying that people would be no worse off if they had to exchange their existing house for one of equal market price but with all other attributes randomly distributed. Most people would feel worse off. This would lead economists to suggest that at least in addition to the market price compensation should also include an element for the net loss in consumers' surplus between the acquired house and one that its owner can purchase at its market value.

The same point can be made in a different way by the use of the concept of *reservation price*. This is the price below which the current owner would withhold the property from the market. You can think of it like a reserve price in an auction: A has a piece of antique furniture which he is willing to sell and he puts it into an auction but tells the auctioneer he is willing to sell it only if the price is greater than £500. Say the bidding stops at £400; since that is below A's reserve price it does not go to the highest bidder because A values it more than he does. (In a sense it does go to the highest bidder, A.)

Where the 'market' price is below A's reservation price A keeps the antique. No one is obliged to sell property at the market price if the reservation price is above it. The point is that for many people the market price for their house is below their reservation price.

The shift in the statutory definition of 'value' brought in by the UK's 1919 Act and repeated in the 1961 Act and implied by US Supreme Court decision in *Monogahela* is precisely this: it rejects reservation price and substitutes market price. This can be seen by a close inspection of rule (ii) of s.5 of the 1961 Act. The value is 'taken to be the amount which the land if sold on the open market by a willing seller might be expected to *realise*'. As Davies points out, this does *not* imply that the seller must be presumed to accept *any* price but it does imply that there is a *willing* buyer. This implies that it is the willing buyer's valuation that determines price, not the seller's reservation price.

Contrast this with the value to the owner principle in effect in the UK prior to 1919. A good clear statement of value to the owner is given by the Canadian Supreme Court in *Diggon-Hibben* v. *the King* in 1949. (The value to the owner criterion was still used in Canada until 1970 since which time six provinces and the federal government have substituted the market price criterion. Four Canadian provinces still retain the value to the owner principle.) The value to the owner principle was stated in this case ([1979] SCR 712 [1949] 4 DLR 785, 64 (CRTC 245)) as meaning: '. . . the owner at the moment of expropriation is to be deemed as without title, but all else remaining the same, and the question is what would he, as a prudent man, at that moment, pay for the property rather than be ejected from it.' This would seem to be at least a first approximation to reservation price.

It should be noted that the market value as defined in the Ontario Expropriations Act of 1980 is 'the amount that the land might be expected to realise if sold in the open market by a willing buyer to a *willing seller*.'

The market value approach totally ignores the fact that an existing owner may have a reservation price above the market price other than from sheer 'bloody-mindedness'.

A third view of this problem is to examine more closely the notion of market price in the context of a unique good like a house. We usually attach significance to the competitive price of a good because that is the price at which the value of an additional unit of the good equals the marginal cost (= opportunity cost) of producing an additional unit of the good.

But the market for a specific property is not the same as that:
output of *that* house cannot be increased. The value of a
specific house to society can be taken to be *at least* what
someone who buys it pays for it but it can also be looked upon
as being what the current owner requires to be paid in order to
give it up, i.e. how much command over resources he requires
to be persuaded to give it up.

Even if no one else is prepared to pay that price (i.e. the
market price is below the reservation price) the reservation
price can still be thought of as the value to society since it
represents the opportunity cost of the owner. If the owner is
unwilling to sell at the highest bidder's price he (the owner) is
implicitly the marginal purchaser and therefore implicitly
society's valuation equals the opportunity cost.

Undoubtedly there is a problem here, in application: anyone
can say that they value their house above its market value.
There is a danger of opportunistic behaviour on the part of the
owner. On the other hand, if there is a market price and the
owner has not sold his property then he presumably values it
at more than the market price. Certainly, if he valued it at less
then the market price would he not have seized the opportunity to sell it, and make himself better off?

There is at least a *prima facie* case that an owner who has
not taken advantage of the market price for his property values
it at more than that market price. As Davies (1984) has
pointed out, there is a paradox at the heart of using 'market
value' as the criterion for compensation in the case of
compulsory purchase:

... 'Market value' as a concept means a purely natural phenomenon, namely
a price level reached between buyers and sellers bargaining with the
minimum of artificial constraints; in theory without any constraints. But this
condition of the 'free market' is the very opposite of the condition of a
compulsory purchase which is *ex hypothesi* a situation of constraint.
Therefore to say that compulsory purchase compensation is to be assessed at
'market value' is to say that a state of affairs is to be visualised in terms of its
direct opposite.

It might be argued that British legislation has recognised this
by the introduction in the Land Compensation Act 1973 of a
'home loss payment'. This may be claimed by someone who

has occupied a substantial part of a compulsory purchased dwelling 'under any interest' for the previous five years. The amount is determined as three times the rateable value of the property but not less than £150 nor more than £1500. I would not regard this as really fitting the bill. It is more like an arbitrary lump-sum to sweeten the bitter pill of compulsion or, as Farrier and McAuslin (1975) call it, a 'sugarplum to tempt people to give up their homes quickly'. It is not based on any attempt to assess the value of the house to its present owner. It's a bit like the 10 per cent of the pre-1919 cases (although likely to be somewhat smaller.)

Perhaps it might be better looked at as a kind of 'solace' compensation for the fact that the sale is compulsory. As such it would be for the intangible consequences of having one's house taken. Farrier and McAuslin argue that it should therefore be based on a sliding-scale related to the length of residence. However, the shock of *compulsion* may be just as great for a new owner as for a long-established owner. What has been argued for so far is not 'solace' compensation but 'equivalency' compensation – compensation for what has been taken. Clearly this is difficult to assess but surely it is arbitrary to say that because it is difficult it should be ignored. Research is needed to find out more about the consumer surplus inherent in house ownership.

The conflict between market value and value to the owner can also be seen as another example of the ask/offer problem discussed in Chapter 3. There, when discussing the Coase theorem, it was pointed out that experimental evidence suggested that people usually required a much higher level of compensation to put up with the loss of an amenity than they were prepared to pay to retain it. This suggests that the compensation for the loss of a house necessary to leave the owner as well off as he was with the house will be greater than he would be willing to pay to keep the house. This means that the measure of compensation given in the *Diggon-Hibben* case is likely to be an under estimate.

Note that the experimental evidence relates to sums of money that are small relative to the wealth of the individual concerned. Might it not be likely that where we are dealing with the value of an asset that is a very high proportion of the individual's wealth that these divergences would be greater i.e. wealth effects are likely to be very 'significant'? Most jurisdictions make clear that 'market value' is not only not the value to the owner but neither is it the value to the taker (condemnor). (For the UK see Davies (1984); for the US, Freilich and Dierker (1975); and for Canada, Knetsch (1983).) Some controversy surrounds this 'value to the taker' principle, as Knetsch calls it. It is often referred to as the *Pointe Gourde* rule after a case where a quarry in Trinidad was compulsorily purchased in order to build a USA air base during World War II. The owner sought additional compensation because of the value of the stone on the land in building the base since otherwise the stone would have had to be brought a great distance. It was argued, however, that the value of the stone was already taken account of in the market value of the quarry, therefore no other purchaser would be willing to pay more than that price for the quarry (including the stone).

The issue here is really quite fundamental to the whole notion of compulsory purchase and eminent domain. Why does it exist? Is it so that public authorities can acquire land more cheaply than private bodies with a similar demand? If it were it would be an unsound economic principle. It would imply that land did not flow to its most highly valued use and consequently would be inefficiently allocated. It would lead to a bias in the input mix for public projects to the extent that other factors of production could be substituted for land.

It has been argued above that compulsory purchase powers are needed because of the high transaction costs associated with bargaining over a specific piece of land or group of pieces of land. Consider the choice of the route for a motorway for which the gross social benefit is £1000 million. This sum would represent the value of faster journeys, savings in fuel, reduced pollution for the journeys made on it as opposed to using existing roads. Once the route of the motorway is decided the owner of each piece of land involved has an incentive to refuse a price which all other owners have accepted, i.e. he would be able to demand up to the full value of the project. Since each owner has such an incentive each one would hold out and no voluntary bargain would be possible. Compulsory purchase substitutes a judicially imposed bargain for a market bargain that cannot be achieved. Notice that the need for compulsory purchase is therefore regardless of whether the motorway is publicly owned or a privately owned toll road. This is why compulsory purchase powers are available for local authorities to acquire land for private shopping redevelopment, urban renewal projects, etc. Indeed in the nineteenth century they were used to acquire land for privately-owned railways. Davies (1984) points out that the earliest examples of compulsory purchase were for enclosures which were for (direct) private benefit.

Now the question at issue is whether the private acquirer of land pays the pre-existing price for the land that he wants or has to pay more. It depends on the particular suitability of the land for his purpose.

Consider the choice of land to set up a factory to build oil rigs because a new oilfield has been discovered off the east coast of Scotland. Let us suppose that a certain area of land adjacent to water of a certain depth is required, the transport cost of a completed oil rig is £10,000 per mile and there is one suitable site on the east coast 30 miles from the oilfield and six sites on the west coast 150 miles from the oilfield. Let us further suppose that each site is currently used for agricultural purpose with a value of £60,000. How much should the fabricator be willing to pay to acquire the site on the east coast?: £1.2 million i.e. $(150-30) \times 10,000$.

Notice that this value is only obtained because of the particular suitability to the acquirer's purpose *combined* with the lack of suitable alternative sites. Whether the owner of the east coast site asks for £60,000 or £1 million does not affect the allocation of resources unless the profits from building the rig are less than £1 million. What it affects is the distribution of profits between oil rig builders and owners of land adjacent to deep water.

On the other hand, if there were six east coast sites equidistant from the field it is likely that the land would sell for only marginally more than its agricultural values because the landowners would compete to make the sale.

How much is paid for the land in the first instance is a question of bargaining skills of the parties concerned (including what information the landowner has about the cost of transporting oil rigs). All that can be said is that the purchase price will be between £60,000 (the price of the land in its next best use) and £1.2 million (the additional cost to the yard of using an alternative site).

Suppose now that the acquirer is not a private company but a public body with compulsory purchase powers (all other facts remaining the same). Should the market value of the agricultural land be £60,000, £1.2 million or what? (We can assume for the purpose of this example that the land concerned is so remote that even with assumed planning permission for industrial use it would still only fetch £60,000.) As the law of compulsory purchase in the UK and the US stands the market value would be assessed at £60,000. To an economist this seems unjust. Compulsory purchase powers are being used to drive down the price of land. In assessing the acquisition price under compulsory purchase some account should be taken of the fact that the project itself increases the demand for land and that not every transaction takes place at the vendor's reservation price. Account must be taken of the alternatives open to the acquiring authority.

In the *Pointe Gourde* case, for example, a great deal would depend on the availability of alternative sites with or without suitable rock. Suppose there were another site available similar in all respects except that it would still need the rock from the Pointe Gourde quarry. Thus the acquiring authority saves *at least* the transport cost of the rock (assuming that the value of the rock is equal to the difference between the market price of the alternative and the market price of the Pointe Gourde quarry). A freely negotiated price for Pointe Gourde would result in its owners obtaining some of the acquirers' saving in transport costs as producers' surplus.

The argument here really is that a judicially (or statutorily) enforced bargain should take into account market realities of supply and demand and not assume that the acquirer's demand is not an influence on market price.

This view is sharpened by considering a Canadian case, *Fraser* v. *the Queen* ([1963] SCR 45J D.L.R2d 707). This involved a project to build a causeway between Cape Breton Island and Nova Scotia. Fraser's site was not the site of the causeway but was acquired because it was the most convenient source of rock and would save the cost of shipping the material from quarries more distant. The initial compensation offer valued the land as wasteland since in the absence of the causeway there was no market for the rock. The compulsory purchase powers are essentially being used to acquire the rock at below the market price for rock. The initial offer was for $5505. The owner originally claimed $5 million + 10 per cent for the taking being compulsory. It was reduced to $1 million + 10 per cent when the acquiring authority reduced the amount of land from 110 to 12.8 acres (this suggests that the cheapness of the land led to an over-taking).

Presumably, given the owner's claim, the cost of bringing materials from the next best source was prohibitive. It might be that that cost was so high that it outweighed the benefits from the project, i.e. the causeway would only be built if materials could be obtained from Fraser's land. This suggests that the bargaining range was between $5505 and the net benefits of the project. Whilst the latter price might seem like extortion it is a *potential* market price. Fraser would probably have settled for much less.

In this particular case an award of $360,000 was made (based, it would seem, on the value of the rock but not taking account of transport costs of what was the acquirer's next best option).

Knetsch points out another reason for the compulsory acquisition price being above the existing use price: the need to preserve property of greater value to society than its existing use, e.g. archaeological sites, listed buildings, etc. If the best that the owner can hope for is the value in existing use there is no incentive to the owner to preserve them. Indeed there is every incentive to hide their existence or allow them to deteriorate. Some kind of bounty or bonus payment might provide such encouragement.

Limiting compensation to existing use values may raise problems of horizontal equity. Davies refers to *Wilson* v. *Liverpool City Council* ([1971] All ER 628, [1971] 1 WLR 302) where land was acquired for a council housing scheme at £4600 per acre. Immediately on the announcement of the scheme an adjacent piece of land was sold to a developer for

£6700 per acre. The higher price reflecting the fact that sewerage works, etc. would be available because of the council scheme. Why should one landowner benefit from the scheme and the other suffer? In this particular case the problem may not be so much one of flaws in compulsory purchase law as one of the system of charging or not charging private developers for connecting their developments to the sewerage system. It looks as 'though the sole difference in the prices is due to the sewerage system already existing and therefore reducing the cost of developing the land. This is being captured in part (or in whole) by the owner of the second piece of land.'

The analysis of this section supports the view that the principles of valuation underlying compulsory purchase in the UK and eminent domain in the United States seem designed more to acquire land cheaply for public bodies than to replace market failure with a judicially determined bargain. Thus they are likely to lead to an inefficient allocation of resources and be unjust.

7 Tort

Tort law is that part of the common law that redresses civil wrongs, usually by compelling the wrong-doer to pay damages or, in the case of nuisance, by an injunction restraining him from continuing the wrong. It embraces, *inter alia*, the areas of negligence, nuisance, trespass and defamation. Modern North American tort scholarship has been heavily influenced by economics. Fletcher has written: 'the fashionable questions of the time are instrumental: what value does the rule of liability further in the case? Does it advance a desirable goal, such as risk distribution or the minimization of accident costs?'

What is involved here is going beyond broad statements about economic efficiency to detailed examination of the economic implications of legal doctrines and remedies. Does the tort system produce a pattern of activity which would be associated with an efficient allocation of resources; or at least does it bring society closer to such an allocation than would alternative systems such as taxation or regulation. This is what is often described as *normative* law-and-economics. However, it is more accurately termed *prescriptive* law-and-economics: it suggests what sort of rules should be used *if* economic efficiency is the goal of the legal system without necessarily arguing that efficiency *should* be the goal of the legal system.

The modern economic approach to tort focuses on its deterrence role. A second role of the tort system is that of providing for a means of the recovery of *compensation* by victims. Thus an evaluation of the compensation role of the tort system might be concerned with the extent to which victims of a tort are able to obtain compensation comparable to the harm caused. In the past, the economics of tort really focused on compensation but in the last two decades it has become almost exclusively concerned with deterrence.

One of the path-breaking studies in the development of this economic approach to tort was that by Guido Calabresi in *The Costs of Accidents* (1970). Calabresi argues that apart from the requirement for justice the principal function of accident law is to *reduce the sum of the costs of accidents and the costs of avoiding accidents.* To this end he identifies three sub-goals:

(i)   Reduction in the number and severity of accidents. This could be achieved either by *forbidding* activities which give rise to them or by making these activities *less attractive* and thereby inducing a substitution away from them to other activities.

(ii) A reduction in the societal costs resulting from accidents, including compensation of victims. This can be achieved by *risk-spreading* or *deep pocket* (making those who can most afford it, pay).

(iii) Reduction in the costs of administering the treatment of accidents. This is the ultimate efficiency objective since there is no point in achieving (i) and (ii) if the cost of doing so exceeds the benefit.

It must also be recognised that the sub-goals may conflict, as indeed the third suggests. Further, society may wish to discourage accident-prone activities but not to the extent that it discourage them below the level at which they can be carried out safely. In such a case specific prohibition would cost more than it would save; e.g. drivers cause accidents but we would presumably not wish to ban driving completely since there are substantial benefits, and not every journey by every driver results in an accident. What has to be achieved is the best combination of the three types of cost reduction taking account of what must be given up to attain them. Calabresi identifies two broad ways of doing this.

(a)   *Specific deterrence* or the *collective approach.* Society collectively decides which activities or levels of activity are to be discouraged and discourages them by penalising their occurrence, e.g. setting of speed limits, compulsory wearing of seat belts, etc.

(b) *General or market deterrence*: this does not involve *a priori* collective decisions as to the correct number of accidents but involves discouraging them by imposing their cost on someone.

Calabresi argues that accident costs should be treated like any other costs which should be weighed by individuals when deciding how much of an activity to undertake. This is advantageous because:

(i) it encourages individuals to engage in *safer activities* by providing an incentive to do so;

(ii) it encourages individuals to make a *given activity safer*.

Consider an example: assume that after two years' normal wear and tear car brakes become unreliable. Society could prohibit the use of brakes more than two years old (specific deterrence) or it could provide an incentive by making drivers whose brakes are more than two years old liable for the cost of any accident caused. In the second case a driver whose brakes were two years old would have to decide whether it was worth replacing them or not. Say the cost of installing new brakes was £100 he would be encouraged to replace them if he thought it likely that he would cause damage greater than £100 (or at least whose expected value was greater than £100). If the expected damage was less than £100 he would not replace the brakes but pay for any damage caused. Under a regime of specific deterrence he would buy the brakes costing £100 and avoid damages of less than £100. Thus resources would have been used where the marginal benefit to society did not exceed their marginal cost.

There are clearly some problems here, e.g. knowing what value of accidents the motorist would have caused. But note also that under a regime of general deterrence there is an incentive for someone to design or develop brakes whose safe life exceeds two years because that would reduce the accident costs borne by drivers. Under specific deterrence there would be no incentive.

A pure market approach to primary accident cost avoidance would require allocation of accident costs to those acts or activities which could avoid accidents most cheaply:

This is the same as saying that the system would allocate the costs to those acts or activities that an arbitrary initial bearer of accident costs would (in the absence of transaction or information costs) find it worthwhile to 'bribe' in order to obtain that modification of behaviour which would lessen accident costs most. (Calabresi)

This is just a statement of the Coase theorem – in the absence of transaction costs it does not matter who initially bears the liability of accident costs.

Transactions are however prohibitively expensive due to the large numbers of motorists and pedestrians and the impossibility of *ex ante* bargains taking place. Thus accident costs cannot be avoided by society. However, another allocation of resources might reduce accident costs and the aim of this approach is to determine the *least-cost avoider*.

A number of possible rules on which tort law might stand will now be examined. This to some extent follows the evolution of such rules in common law jurisdictions. The rules are:

(i) *Strict liability*: Under strict liability the injurer must compensate the victim. This principle was eroded in the nineteenth century on both sides of the Atlantic in response to the plea for 'no liability without fault', and the increasing number of accidents brought about in the wake of industrialisation. This has led to the so-called 'judicial subsidy theory' (see Horwitz (1977); and Friedman (1973), Part III, Ch VI).

(ii) *Negligence*: The injurer is only liable for damage for negligent acts. The standard of care there is that of a 'reasonable man'.

(iii) *Contributory negligence*: A defence based on the victim himself having negligently contributed to the accident.

(iv) *Comparative negligence*: A rule based on the idea that both injurer and victim should be liable in proportion to their contribution to the accident through negligent behaviour.

STRICT LIABILITY AND NEGLIGENCE

Consider the following stylised example illustrated in Figure 7.1 where the accident rate (negative of care) produces an increasing marginal cost on the victim and an increasing marginal cost (of care) on the injurer.

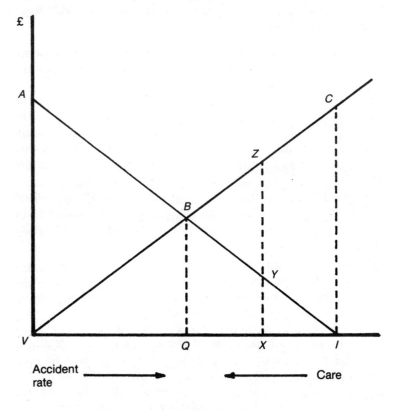

Figure 7.1

If accident bargaining were possible the optimal accident rate would be Q where the marginal benefit of accident prevention (which is the avoided costs to the victim) equals the marginal cost of accident prevention. Under the Coase theorem this would be attained whoever had the initial rights (or entitlement): victim or injurer.

Under *strict liability* the entitlement is with the victim and the injurer must pay for any damage caused. Expenditure on care starting from I in Figure 7.1 is justified for the injurer since it costs him less than the compensation would, e.g. by reducing the accident rate to X at a cost IXY saving costs of $ICZX$, i.e. a net gain of $ICZY$. There will be such a net gain until the accident rate is reduced to Q: the *cost-justified accident level*. The injurer will still have to pay compensation VBQ to the victims. There is a net gain to society (over no care) of IBC.

Strict liability would induce the potential injurer to take the efficient level of care, resulting in the optimal number (or the cost-justified level) of accidents. Strict liability is also Pareto superior in the sense that no one is left worse off as a result of the accident-generating activity.

From the mid-nineteenth century strict liability was gradually replaced in most common law jurisdictions by *negligence*: 'Negligence is conduct falling below the standard established for the protection of others against unreasonable risk of harm. This standard of conduct is ordinarily measured by what the reasonable man of ordinary prudence would do in the circumstances' (Fleming (1968), p. 106). The identification of behaviour as 'negligent' implies no moral connotation. It is in essence a practical test. The 'reasonable man' is an 'objective standard'. It therefore avoids the need to judge each individual's subjective capacity, but on the other hand, allows flexibility from situation to situation and from time to time. Being objective it was also easily communicable to a jury. However, in the UK juries no longer sit in negligence trials.

It should, however, be recognised that the reasonable man standard does not mean that mere customary behaviour may not be found negligent, otherwise an industry, for example, could lower its standard of care by uniformly lowering its customary practice. The 'reasonable man' can also vary from circumstance to circumstance. Thus the standard of care required of a surgeon is in essence that of a 'reasonable surgeon'. (Although some authorities might argue that the law has been over-considerate of its brother profession.)

Negligent behaviour does not necessarily imply liability. The defendant must also owe the victim a duty of care. Such duty will depend on the relation between the parties (e.g. a trespasser is not owed a duty of care), the nature of the conduct that caused the harm (e.g. failure to rescue does not give rise to liability), and the nature of the injury (e.g. subjective harm such as fright is not usually recognised).

To succeed in an action for damages a plaintiff (*Donoghue v. Stevenson* [1932]) would have to establish that:

(i)   the defendant owed him a duty of care;
(ii) in breaching that duty the defendant behaved negligently;
(iii) the damage to the plaintiff resulted from that breach.

All of these can be infused with an economic content: (i) is a question of property rights, (ii) implies a causal link, (iii) may seem somewhat problematic but if examined closely it can be seen to have more than a little economic content. As Fleming (1968) says, this is based on a 'delicate balancing of competing considerations'. This

calculus of risk may at best be reduced to the formula that we must weigh the magnitude of risk in the light of the likelihood of an accident happening and the possible seriousness of its consequence against the difficulty, expense, or another disadvantage of desisting from the venture or taking a particular precaution. (p. 33)

A leading case in England on this matter is *Bolton v. Stone* ([1951] AC850 (HL)) which decision is discussed in Lord Reid's speech in *Overseas Tankship (UK) Ltd v. The Miller Steamship Co. Pty (Wagon Mound No 2)* ([1967] 1AC 617 at 641 (HL)):

... The House of Lords held that the risk was so small that in the circumstances a reasonable man would have been justified in disregarding it and taking no steps to eliminate it.

But it does not follow that, no matter what the circumstances may be, it is justifiable to neglect a risk of such a small magnitude. A reasonable man would only neglect such a risk if he had some valid reason for doing so, eg that it would involve considerable expenses to eliminate the risk. He would weigh the risk against the difficulty of eliminating it.

This looks suspiciously like a weighing of the costs and benefits of alternative courses of action – not to the injurer but to the injurer *and* the victim: In short, a judicial balancing of the costs and benefits.

The apogee of this judicial cost-benefit analysis is in the judgment of Judge Learned Hand in *US* v. *Carrol Towing Co.* (159 F2d 169 [2d Circuit, 1947]) who, when discussing the liability of an owner for an unattended barge breaking from its mooring and damaging other vessels, said:

... the owner's duty ... is a function of three variables: (1) the probability that she will break away; (2) the gravity of the resulting injury, if she does; (3) the burden of adequate precautions ... if the probability be called P; the injury, L; and the burden, B; liability depends upon whether ... $B < PL$

B, of course, is the cost of avoidance and PL is the expected cost of the accident. Strictly speaking the expectation is $\Sigma p_i L_i$ where each of the L_i is a potential outcome and p_i is its probability. In the Hand formula there are only two outcomes, L and 0, with probabilities P and $(1-P)$ yielding an expected value of $p.L + (1-P). 0 = P.L.$

The Hand formula does not provide a complete economic rule because it is expressed in terms of *total* costs and benefits not *marginal* costs and benefits. What is required is an *incremental* Hand test, i.e. we should be concerned with the marginal costs and benefits of different precautions.

It would seem that judges, including Hand, think in terms of one form of precaution and therefore the choice is between doing nothing and doing something. In most cases there will be a range of precautions that might have been taken (even if they consist of going 1 m.p.h. slower, 2 m.p.h. slower, etc.). The optimal level of precaution will therefore be where:

$$\Delta B = p\Delta L$$

i.e. marginal cost of avoidance = marginal expected benefit of avoidance. This economic interpretation of the incremental Hand formula would thus result in the socially optimal level of care, i.e. negligence as the standard of care (properly interpreted) would be efficient. The 'reasonable man' in the interpretation would only take cost-justified precautions, i.e. he would not take precautions for which

$$mc > mb$$

(Notice that in a world of economically rational potential injurers, where the incremental Hand formula was used to determine liability, no negligent accidents would take place. Some accidents would take place but they would be cost-justified.)

In terms of Figure 7.1 the potential injurer would take precautions reducing the accident rate to Q since an accident above Q would make him liable to damages in excess of his benefits, e.g. $QBZX > QBYX$. By operating at Q the injurer would avoid any liability for damages. It should be noted that in this analysis the level of activity is predetermined and only the care taken is variable. The victim would suffer damage of VBQ but would not receive any compensation because it is more efficient to have accidents than to avoid them. Once again this is a Coasian result that in terms of efficiency it does not matter which tort rule is used (strict liability or negligence) the optimal level of care (or accident rate) results. The difference between the two rules is in their distributional consequences. Under strict liability the costs of accidents are borne by injurers whilst under negligence they are borne by victims.

Veljanovski (1981) discusses the notion of corrective justice as well as that of distributive justice in the context of tort rules. Distributive justice will determine with whom the entitlement should lie – victim or injurer. Epstein (1979) has defined corrective justice as 'rendering to each person whatever redress is required because of the violation of his rights by others'. Veljanovski argues that strict liability implies an entitlement (distributive justice) lying with the victim, whereas under negligence it lies with the injurer. He then demonstrates, using the fiction of a hypothetical bargain between injurer and victim, that under either liability rule the party not assigned the initial entitlement does better than he would have done had bargaining been feasible. Thus neither rule fully satisfies the requirements of corrective justice in that the party whose right is infringed is not compensated to the same extent that he would be under a bargain. However, Veljanovski's analysis presumes polar entitlements.

Thus far it has been assumed that the level of care is the determinant of the number of accidents but it will also be a function of the injurer's level of participation in the accident-generating activity. For example, the number of car accidents will be determined not only by driver care but also by the number of miles driven. Under strict liability where the injurer bears all accident costs he can reduce these not only by taking more care but by reducing the number of miles driven. Thus, then, he must internalise accident costs into his decision on whether or not a journey is worthwhile as well as whether a certain level of care is worthwhile. Strict liability should therefore generate the efficient level of participation in the activity. Negligence, on the other hand, would not seem to affect the degree of participation in the activity. The negligence standard of reasonableness would seem to relate only to the conditions under which the activity is carried out not whether it should be carried out as frequently or not. For example, negligence only relates to the care used by the driver in the circumstances of a particular journey, not on the number of journeys the driver makes. Therefore, where the degree of participation in the accident-generating activity is a significant determinant of the number of accidents a rule of strict liability is more likely to generate the efficient level of accidents than one of negligence.

Administrative costs of settling disputes were also identified above as a cost of accidents. These will depend on the number of such disputes and the cost of resolving each one. The number of litigated disputes is likely to be higher under strict liability than under negligence since the latter provides an incentive for injurers to take care. However, the costs of deciding each litigated case will be higher under negligence since the behaviour of the injurer must be investigated and compared to the standard of care. Under strict liability only the damage done need be ascertained. Thus efficiency does not unambiguously favour one rule or the other.

CONTRIBUTORY AND COMPARATIVE NEGLIGENCE

In the discussion so far it has been implicitly assumed that only actions by the injurer can reduce the number of accidents. However, very often the 'victim' is in a position to reduce the probability of an accident by himself taking care. This gave rise to the defence of contributory negligence, i.e. that the plaintiff was negligent himself in not taking some action which a reasonable man would have taken to prevent the accident. Since the plaintiff's negligence has contributed to the accident how can the defendant be held liable for it? An early case in the evolution of this doctrine is that of *Butterfield* v. *Forrester* ([1809] KB 103 ER 926).

In the absence of a defence which makes the plaintiff's actions relevant the problem of what economists call *moral hazard* arises: the plaintiff shifts the burden of his failure to take due care onto someone else. We can see why this would not be efficient by considering a situation where the plaintiff is the least-cost avoider. Say an accident with an expected cost of £100 could be avoided by the defendant spending £30 in taking extra care. The defendant would be found negligent. However, if the plaintiff could have avoided the accident at a cost to himself of £20 a negligence rule would be inefficient since it would induce an expenditure of £30 of resources to avoid an outcome which could have been avoided by only spending £20 of resources. The defence of contributory negligence can be seen as a means to overcome this moral hazard problem. The plaintiff is induced to take 'reasonable' care.

Notice that such a defence is equally applicable when the rule is one of strict liability. Why should the defendant be strictly liable for the effects of an accident which the plaintiff could have avoided more cheaply? Thus where the victim's care is relevant a rule of strict liability with contributory negligence will be efficient.

A negligence rule with contributory negligence would be efficient if the plaintiff was the least-cost avoider. However, if the defendant is the least-cost avoider a defence of contributory negligence would not be efficient.

It should be noted here that this analysis (based on the least-cost avoider principle) presumes one or other party can completely avoid the accident, i.e. it does not require joint care, nor does care by both further reduce accident damage.

Whilst a defence of contributory negligence may be efficient when the plaintiff is the least-cost avoider it does not mean that it should be a universal defence, as it became in the nineteenth century. In many jurisdictions the slightest element of negligence on the part of the plaintiff to take reasonable care was sufficient to defeat the action. Thus even if the defendant were the cheapest-cost avoider, the plaintiff bore the full cost of the accident if he were negligent to the slightest extent. Put in, perhaps, more familiar terms, even if the plaintiff were only 10 per cent responsible for the accident and the defendant 90 per cent responsible the plaintiff bore all the costs. This inequitable effect of contributory negligence was softened, in many instances, by the doctrine of 'last clear chance' whereby responsibility lay with the party who had the last opportunity to avoid the accident (frequently the injurer). The all-or-nothing element of contributory negligence could also mean that where a plaintiff was in effect responsible in some degrees for the accident but the burden fell on the defendant because he had the 'last clear chance' to avoid it the plaintiff would receive 100 per cent compensation for an accident for which, in some measure, he had helped cause. A way round this was found by juries who (where a range of damages was available) settled on damages towards the lower end of the permissible range.

An intuitively plausible solution would be to adopt a rule that apportioned liability for an accident between plaintiff and defendant in proportion to their negligence or responsibility for it. This is the rule of *comparative negligence* which in one form or another is now applicable in many jurisdictions (including England and Scotland and a number of US states). It has often been brought about by legislation rather than judicial decisions (although seven US states did adopt it judicially).

Some economists (or economist/lawyers) have dismissed comparative negligence as inefficient when compared to contributory negligence (e.g. Posner, Brown). This has been challenged in a recent paper by Haddock and Curran (1985). They argue that Posner's criticism of comparative negligence is ill-founded because it assumes that either party can wholly remove the accident and that both parties taking the efficient level of care is wasteful since one party having taken it there are no incremental gains from the other party taking it also. This may not be the case.

Brown's (1973) formulation of efficiency does assume that both parties need to take care and is attained by minimising the care costs of potential defendants, the care costs of potential plaintiffs and residual accident costs. Thus tort law seeks to

$$\text{Min } C(X, Y) = w^x X + w^y Y + A[1 - P(X, Y)]$$
$$X, Y$$

where X and Y are the care levels of defendant and plaintiff which have unit costs w^x and w^y, $C(X, Y)$ is social costs, A is the accident cost, and $P(X, Y)$ is the probability of an accident given X and Y.

The optimal level of care is attained where w^x or w^y equals marginal benefit. Brown assumes A is constant and that it is P that falls as care increases and that comparative negligence means that the cost of accidents will be shared. This will induce each party to reduce care below the optimum level.

Haddock and Curran argue that a comparative negligence rule only apportions the burden when both parties are negligent. If the defendant is not negligent he bears no cost, if he was negligent and the plaintiff was not the defendant bears all the burden. Contributory negligence places all burden on the plaintiff if he is negligent regardless of the defendant's actions. Thus even if the defendant is negligent the plaintiff bears all the burden.

If the courts are knowledgeable enough to set the legal standard of care (X^*, Y^*) at the efficient level (X^o, Y^o) Haddock and Curran call the negligence rule 'full-cost negligence'. Negligence with contributory negligence may be seen to produce an efficient degree of care because if $X = X^*$ the plaintiff's best strategy is to set $Y = Y^o*$, and conversely if $Y = Y^*$ defendants best strategy is to set $X = X^o*$. Thus the efficient levels of care (X^o, Y^o) are a stable equilibrium if selected as the legal standard of care when the rule is full-cost negligence with contributory negligence.

Thus full-cost negligence with contributory negligence is efficient. This is illustrated in Figure 7.2, which is adapted from Curran and Haddock (1985). Both parties choose the efficient level of care. Note the discontinuity in the defendant's costs when he falls below reasonable care.

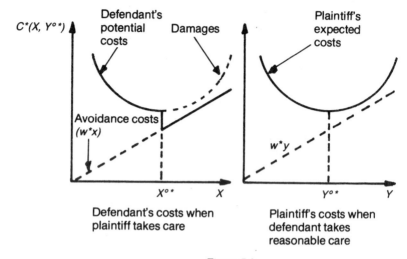

Figure 7.2

Comparative negligence can take two forms: the so-called 'pure' form where regardless of the degree of negligence each party bears his share of the burden, and the so-called 50 per cent rule whereby if more than 50 per cent of the accident is due to the plaintiff's negligence he bears all the costs. Haddock and Curran examine comparative negligence, first by seeing if $(X^{o}{*}, Y^{o}{*})$ is a stable position under either form. If either party is meeting the legal standard the other party minimises his costs by meeting the legal standard of care. Thus if parties expect socially optimal behaviour from each other they will themselves behave optimally.

The second question they ask is if neither party is taking the optimum level of care will either rule of comparative negligence induce a move to $(X^{o}{*}, Y^{o}{*})$?

Under the 50 per cent rule the defendant can either be less negligent than the plaintiff and be free of liability; or be more negligent than the plaintiff and save care costs. If the defendant tries to be less negligent than the plaintiff the latter's optimal strategy is to minimise his loss by taking the optimal level of care. If the defendant opts to be more negligent than the plaintiff he leaves himself open to sharing the burden with the plaintiff. The plaintiff's optimal strategy is to be non-negligent and the defendant bears all of the burden, therefore he will choose optimal care.

Under pure comparative negligence the same results obtain. Haddock and Curran then show that there can be no stable planned level of negligence for both parties, i.e. the defence of comparative negligence can only arise if somebody makes a mistake. If one party is negligent it always pays the other party to be non-negligent. Haddock and Curran then go on to examine the situation with error and find contributory negligence is unlikely to be efficient.

In addition to efficiency considerations if fairness carries any weight it is likely to suggest comparative negligence as opposed to contributory negligence. It should be noted, however, that there are some problems with comparative negligence. First, there is more than one way to share liability, e.g. in terms of prevention costs or in terms of net losses caused by the parties' failure to take precautions. Secondly, efficient behaviour under comparative negligence may involve high information costs in determining the prevention possibilities and costs of the other party (although a minimax strategy suggests taking efficient care for both parties).

RISK-AVERSION AND INSURANCE

Our discussion so far in this chapter on tort rules in general and the Hand formula in particular has involved an implicit assumption about the attitude to risk of the parties: that they are *risk-neutral*. It was stated above that the Hand formula seemed to be arguing that the expected value of the damage done should be compared to the costs of avoiding the damage. If the former is the larger then the defendant has behaved negligently.

A generalised version of the Hand formula might be that the defendant has behaved negligently if

$$\Sigma\, p_i L_i > B$$

where L_i is the ith loss and B is the burden of avoiding the loss

$$\text{or } p_1 L_1 + p_2 L_2 + \dots + p_n L_n > B.$$

The *LHS* of this relationship might be called the *expected loss* of the victim. It is the weighted average of all the possible losses that might occur: the weights being their probability of occurrence. These probabilities need not be *objective* probabilities, arrived at by a series of repeated outcomes. They are more likely to be *subjective* probabilities: assessments in the mind of the particular actors concerned.

Implicit in the Hand formula is the assumption that a reasonable man would be indifferent between a burden of adequate precaution (B) and an expected loss of the same magnitude. Will that be the case? How would the 'reasonable man of ordinary prudence' view a gamble with outcomes

$$L_1 = -£50 \qquad P_1 = .2$$
$$L_2 = -£30 \qquad P_2 = .3 \qquad \Sigma p_i L_i = -26.5$$
$$L_3 = -£15 \qquad P_3 = .5$$

or a certain loss of £28?

The Hand formula would seem to suggest that 'a reasonable man' would take the gamble because its expected value is higher than the certain loss. Note, however, that the probability of the loss being greater than £28 is 0.5. Most people would probably take the certain loss of £28 because they are risk-averse, i.e. they demand a risk premium for facing uncertain outcomes. Put another way, most people would not accept a fair gamble whose expected value was the same as a sum they could obtain with certainty. One might say that risk-aversion is the economist's explanation for the old adage that a bird in the hand is worth two in the bush. On the other hand, some people may be risk preferers, i.e. gamblers. They will be willing to take a fair gamble where its expected value is less than a sum they could obtain with certainty.

On the whole, the ordinary man of prudence may well be expected to take the precaution even if the expected loss is less than the burden of avoidance because the reasonable man may be thought to be risk-averse.

It is thus not expected value which is relevant but expected utility. Put more formally behaviour will be deemed negligent if:

$$\sum_i p_i U(L_i) > U(B)$$

where $U(.)$ indicates the utility of the given event. Presumably the relevant utility function is that of the reasonable man of prudence.

Having noted the importance of risk-aversion the next thing to consider is insurance, since people contemplating hazards with (for them) uncertain or unpredictable rates of ocurrence usually turn to insurance to convert uncertain outcomes into certain (in financial terms) ones. The existence of insurance also has implications for the tort system.

Essentially an ideal insurance policy removes the risk to an individual which arises from undertaking a potentially hazardous activity. By taking out insurance the individual forgoes some income (the premium) in order to avoid a possible substantial loss of income (either directly due to injury to himself or indirectly through liability for an injury or loss caused to another person) sometime during the insurance policy's life. The individual now has, *ceteris paribus*, a certain income regardless of whether or not the insured risk actually occurs.

Insurance companies can be profitable because they can pool individual risks across a large number of individual policy-holders. Their actual liability will be the expected value of the losses incurred by their policy-holders. Large organisations involved in a large number of risky activities often do not insure (or at least self-insure) because they can pool risks across their activities. For example, a public transit authority might not insure its vehicles with an insurance company (it might however be bound by compulsory third party insurance laws) because given the large number of vehicles it operates and the large number of miles which they travel it is likely that the total premium they would be charged would exceed the benefits they would receive in terms of vehicle repair costs, i.e. the authority's activities provide a sufficiently large pool to make damage predictable (i.e. actual losses = expected losses).

Insurance, however, gives rise to the problem of 'moral hazard': a fully insured individual has no incentive to take care to avoid the loss and, *ceteris paribus*, insurance may lead to an increase in the number of losses. Notice that large organisations which self-insure will be encouraged to take care because the costs of accidents are internalised to that organisation, i.e. there is no moral hazard.

A consequence of moral hazard is that ideal insurance should not only provide full coverage but premia should reflect the behaviour of the insured. This is difficult to do *ex ante* but can be done *ex post* via no claims bonuses, surcharges for behaviour likely to give rise to higher incidence of claims, e.g. motoring convictions etc., compulsory deductibles and co-insurance (i.e. < 100 per cent coverage). (For a discussion of the economics of moral hazard see Pauly (1968). For a study of how regulation designed to improve safety increases accidents (analogous to the moral hazard problem of insurance) see Pelzman (1978).)

We can therefore see that while insurance may be a necessary complement to the tort system in order that those held liable for a costly accident under a tort regime are able to meet the liability imposed upon them it may actually reduce the deterrent effect of the system because once the premium is paid the incentive to take adequate care is reduced significantly.

Insurance is a form of risk-spreading which in effect involves a spreading of risks across those who participate in a certain activity (e.g. drivers). Risks may be spread further through a system of social insurance. Under such a scheme tort liability would be removed and victims compensated for loss or injury from a fund financed via taxation. Thus risks are spread across all activities and all members of the population. A major benefit of such a scheme is that it reduces administrative costs which arise from litigation where liability needs to be proved. Under a social insurance scheme the administrative costs are those of collecting contributions and ascertaining damage (which has to be done under tort anyway). A drawback of social insurance is that it removes deterrence. A no-fault social insurance scheme operates in New Zealand (see Harris, 1972). For a discussion of the pros and cons of social insurance versus tort by a tort lawyer see Bruce Dunlop (1981).

THE ECONOMIC FORMULATION OF NEGLIGENCE AND THE COURTS

Although the purpose of this chapter is to set forth the prescriptive law-and-economics of tort the reader may be tempted, particularly given the origins of the Hand formula, to go further and conclude that the concept of negligence used in the courts has a high degree of congruence with the economic concept. Such a reader would not be alone. The view that the common law is efficient has been espoused by a number of contributors to the law-and-economics literature. The leading proponent of this view is Richard Posner (formerly Professor of Law at the University of Chicago and at the time of writing a US Federal court judge). The problems of sustaining such a view will be elucidated more fully in Chapter 9. In the present context comment is apposite because it was the study of negligence which first prompted the efficiency claim to be made (see Posner, 1972b). The Hand formula does look very much like how an economist would view the question. It involves a judicial balancing of costs and benefits. The language used by other judges (e.g. the quotation from Lord Reid given earlier) and the comments of legal scholars such as Fleming is in terms of probabilities and likelihoods. However, this similarity of vocabulary should not be taken as indicating an identity of concepts. The formal mathematician's concept of probability which is used by economists is distributional, i.e. the sum of the probabilities must be one. In common usage (including by judges) the term is used more loosely to denote some measure of *possibility* which is not necessarily distributional. Some economists have questioned the use by economists of the distributional concept in the context of decision-making under uncertainty (see, in particular, Shackle, 1952; 1969, 1970). The empirical validity of the expected utility model has been questioned (for a review of this literature, see Schoemaker, 1982). The distributional basis of probability needs close examination in the context of activities giving rise to torts. Posner (1982), in outlining the Hand formula writes, '"expected cost" of the accident ... is the average cost that will be incurred over a period of time long enough for the predicted number of accidents to be the actual number.' He clearly had in mind, as Judge Hand had, the number of occasions when the actual accident would occur. This expected cost was to be compared with the cost of avoiding the accident. Consider now an arithmetical example based on the stylised facts of *Carrol Towing* which involved an unattended barge breaking from its moorings and damaging other vessels. Suppose the actual damage done was $50,000 involving the total destruction of another vessel, and it was estimated that there was only a one in a thousand chance that on any night the conditions would be such as to loose a vessel from its moorings in a way which would so significantly damage another vessel. The 'expected cost' of this accident is $50. Suppose that the cost of employing someone to watch over the vessel is $60. The 'expected cost of the accident' is less than the burden of adequate precautions. Thus on the Hand formula leaving the barge unattended is *not* negligent behaviour.

However, if the question of relevance is whether it was negligent not to employ a watchman surely it is relevant to consider not only the accident that actually occurred but all other consequences of leaving the barge unattended. Suppose that there was a one in a hundred chance that the barge would slip its moorings and cause minor damage to another vessel amounting to $5000. The expected cost of leaving the barge unattended is now:

$$\sum_{i=1}^{2} P_i L_i = 0.001 \times 50,000 + 0.01 \times 5000$$
$$= 50 + 50 = \$100$$

Since the expected cost of leaving the boat unattended now exceeds the burden of adequate precautions it is 'negligent' behaviour. Thus whether only the actual accident or all potential outcomes of the behaviour being evaluated are incorporated in the calculation of 'expected cost' may be of crucial relevance in determining whether the behaviour is, economically-speaking, 'negligent'. Clearly, incorporating 'all potential outcomes' is an impossible burden to put on anyone: an event may be a potential outcome but might occur so infrequently that the defendant could not be expected to be aware of its potential. This is a fundamental problem of the probability-based approach to decision-making under uncertainty. As Shackle (1952) has pointed out, it requires a residual hypothesis, i.e. a probability must be attached to all outcomes of which the decision-maker has not thought. Shackle resolves this problem by moving away from probability to a non-distributional likelihood concept which he calls 'possibility'. It seems to the present writer that when 'probability' is used by judges (including Mr Justice Hand) it is being used in such a non-distributional sense. It is therefore illegitimate to use the term 'expected loss' in the context of judicial decisions on negligence. An efficiency-based criterion for negligence based on the expected value criterion would be as follows (in the context of *Carrol Towing*). 'Failure to provide a watchman at night would be negligent if the sum of the products of the value of the additional accidents occurring and their probability of occurrence exceeded the cost of providing a watchman.' Symbolically it would be indicated by:

$$\sum_i p_i L_i > B$$

where the L_i are the monetary values of a given accident and p_i is its probability of occurrence. This would be equivalent to saying that behaviour is negligent if its expected marginal social cost exceeded its marginal social benefit.

The judicial concept of negligence does not consider the full distribution of possible outcomes of the behaviour under investigation; it focuses on one outcome: that which actually occurred. It asks whether it was reasonable to neglect this outcome; it takes account of the frequency with which it might be thought to occur; it considers the magnitude of the loss; and it considers the cost of avoiding the loss. It is clearly not distributional since it focuses on one class of potential outcome. This bears more than a passing resemblance to Shackle's (1952) analysis of decision-making under uncertainty (although the latter does not wholly explain it). The somewhat negative conclusion of this section must be that the concept of negligent behaviour espoused by the courts does not correspond to the efficiency-based definition of negligence espoused in the literature. However, on the positive side it can be said that it recognises some economic factors.

LIABILITY IN A MARKET SETTING

The discussion of tort has focused, primarily, on accidents: a case where bargains to transfer entitlements are not usually possible *ex ante*. The courts were then seen to be imposing the terms of an efficient bargain *ex post*. There are many situations sounding in tort in which *ex ante* bargains between parties do take place, implicitly if not explicitly. These are situations which Ogus and Veljanovski (1984) refer to as 'Liability in a Market Setting', the principal examples being *product liability* and *employers' liability*. Notice that here the liability bears some relation to a commercial transaction (e.g. the liability of a manufacturer for damage caused by a product which he sold to someone; the liability of an employer for damage caused to an employee in the course of his employment). Contractual relations become of relevance. In fact, in earlier times both were subject to contract remedies, became recognised as torts, and are now to varying degrees the provenance of statutory rather than common law. The common feature in these two fields is that two parties have engaged in a transaction (the sale of a product; the sale of labour) then one of the parties suffers damage (the consumer is injured as a consequence of using the product; the worker is injured in the course of his employment). What liability falls on the other party to make the injured party whole?

The relevance of contract doctrines here, of course, is whether the terms of the transaction took account of the accident potentialities: Was the product cheaper because it was unsafe (neglecting for the moment that the consumer probably transacted with a retailer rather than the manufacturer)? Was the worker paid a higher wage because it was a dangerous occupation? The courts here might be seen as reflecting a sort of neoclassical market-oriented doctrine that price is a reflection of the terms of a bargain – the more you expect to get from the exchange the more you should expect to pay. (Of course the employee's payment in this context is negative. See for example McKean (1970).)

Consider product liability. A number of interesting questions are raised here. To whom should manufacturers be liable for the defects of their products? What, indeed, constitutes a defect? Should manufacturers be responsible for all 'defects' in their products including those that could not reasonably be foreseen? Should manufacturers be strictly liable for defects or should negligence be required? Should contracts be subject to implied warranties or not? We cannot hope to deal here with all of these questions but shall concern ourselves mainly with those that are susceptible to economic reasoning.

It may seem strange to us now but for many years (though not in Scotland) a manufacturer's liability was restricted to those with whom he had a contractual relationship (privity). Thus, for example, the bottler of a fizzy drink, would not have been held liable for the damage to a bystander's eye caused by an exploding bottle sold to someone else. Indeed, even if the injured party were the purchaser his action would have lain not against the bottler but against the vendor. Of course, a chain of liability would extend all the way back to the manufacturer of the bottle but this required separate actions and could be broken by explicit contractual terms or a disclaimer at any point. This seems indefensible if for no other reason than it would imply very high administrative costs associated with the large number of court cases that would arise from a simple incident. Looked at from a deterrence perspective it might produce the wrong signals: either (i) no one along the chain need take care because it would be possible to pass the cost on to the party at the next stage back along the chain if liability was strict; or avoid liability because of the difficulty of the party at the next stage forward proving negligence or avoiding contributory negligence; or (ii) there would be too much care taken at each stage because of a fear that it might not be possible to shift liability backwards.

(Notice that if transaction costs were zero it would not matter who was legally liable because costless bargaining between the parties would lead to an efficient set of contracts emerging (the Coase theorem). Of course, in most instances transaction costs would not be zero.)

Previous discussion would suggest that economic efficiency dictates that liability falls on the least-cost avoider of the harm. In many instances this is likely to be the manufacturer. He will have the necessary information about the product and its manufacture and is in a better position than the consumer to safeguard adulteration during production, etc. However, circumstances can arise where the purchaser may be the least-cost avoider, e.g. where it is the conditions under which it is used which make the product dangerous (abnormal use defence).

The law in England changed with the judgment in *Donoghue v. Stevenson* ([1932] AC 562). (Plaintiff allegedly suffered injury as a result of consuming ginger ale bought for her by a friend. The bottle was found to contain the decomposed remains of a snail.) This case widened a manufacturer's duty of care to all foreseeable users of the manufacturer's product.

The duty of care does not fall exclusively on the manufacturer but 'all who in the process of design, manufacture and distribution make "the thing" a source of foreseeable peril to others' (Fleming (1968), p. 93). Fleming points out that retailers would be expected to provide fewer safeguards than manufacturers (except where conditions of storage may make the product dangerous). Fleming offers a least-cost argument here. Manufacturers, however, could shift responsibility to retailers by a suitably worded warning notice to the latter to test the good adequately.

Another point made by Flemming reintroduces the market argument: some goods ('seconds') may be sold on the specific understanding that they are defective or even dangerous. There is a duty on the seller to ensure that the buyer is aware of the defects and the risks in which they might involve him. Having discharged that duty, liability thereafter falls on the buyer for any consequent damage.

(A discussion of the arguments used in the leading US case, *Escola v. Coca Cola Bottling Co. of Fresno* ([1944] 150 Pd), to justify the introduction of strict liability (incentive, hardship, insurance and administrative costs) is given in Epstein (1980), who argues that, other than administrative costs, none of the arguments justifies strict liability over negligence.)

McKean (1970) points out that a shift from *caveat emptor* to *cavet venditor* will involve a change in property rights, a change in the costs of products and perhaps the removal of some products from the market to the detriment of some consumers. McKean's paper is a good statement of the market-oriented position that regulation restricts consumer choice by paternalism. Essentially this analysis conceives of the situation as one of joint production and joint consumption: two goods are being produced and sold – the commodity itself and safety. Different people will differ in the 'quantity' of safety they demand in combination with the 'commodity'. The quantity of safety demanded will be a function of income, i.e. it is a normal good (indeed, it may be a luxury good) therefore less of it will be demanded by the poor than by the rich.

Regulation of product quality or safety may increase the 'quantity' of safety incorporated in the good (possibly because the better-off have a greater demand for it). This will increase the cost of production and raise price. The poor will be faced with having to consume more safety than they are willing to pay for and will switch to the consumption of other goods. The rich will get a quantity of safety which they could have obtained via the market, but the poor will be denied the good.

Walter Oi (1973) has challenged this view on the grounds that it is the full price of the risky good (actual price and expected losses) that is relevant. If average compensation is less than the expected losses to the marginal consumer a change to *caveat venditor* will lower price.

It should be noted that the law of contract and the law of tort have developed separate tests for what might be called *defectiveness*. In the product liability context contractual remedies usually arise from a test of whether or not the product was 'of merchantable quality' or 'fit for its purpose', both of which can be interpreted in terms of consumer expectations which are ascertainable in the terms of the bargain. Under contract law the disappointed party can get compensation for the difference between the value of the product and its value had it complied with reasonable expectations. In negligence, liability is predicated on a breach of a duty of care. This involves the conduct of the producer (rather than condition of product) and societal interests (rather than consumer's expectations). Foreseeable costs and benefits are weighed and if benefits are outweighed liability ensues.

The distinction between contract and tort bases of liability in this area has gradually been eroded in both the United

States and the United Kingdom. The two bases of liability are joined in S402A of The Restatement (Second) of Torts (see also Montgomery and Owen, 1976) and the decision in *Junior Books Ltd* v. *Veitchi Co. Ltd* ([1982] 3 All ER 201) where damages were awarded in tort for purely financial losses caused by a defective product (see further Clark, 1985). These may be viewed as importing into the law of tort a manufacturer's warranty that goods are merchantable and as fit for their purpose as the exercise of reasonable care could make them. Such developments do not seem as strange to an economist as they appear to be to some legal commentators since the former approaches most questions in a more general way than the latter with their compartmentalised view of what the law is. However subsequent judgments have restricted *Junior Books* to its facts.

This discussion of 'liability in a market setting' leads naturally to the subject-matter of the next chapter: the law of contract.

8 Contract

In a sense the law of contract should be the one area of the law
where economic analysis is most relevant. After all, economics
is largely the study of exchanges – *Catellactics*. Most of what
we call neoclassical economics is about market transactions.
The law of contract is the body of law which surrounds such
exchanges. However, neoclassical economics has until recently
had little to say about contract. It has simply assumed that
there exists a body of law or conventions that ensures that
transactions take place. In many ways the benefits are flowing
in the other direction. A greater awareness by economists of
the complexity, sophistication and variety of contractual
relations is having a considerable impact on the evolution of
economic thought.

Let us begin by considering why exchanges take place. It
comes naturally to an economist to say that they do so because
both parties to the exchange are made better off: A has a
widget, B needs a widget and values it more than A does; they
exchange the widget for some consideration and both are
better off; A has something which is worth more to him than
the widget; B has the widget which is worth more to him than
what he gave up. The exchange has increased value (or more
properly utility) and is desirable. Value-enhancing exchanges
should be encouraged and facilitated if we wish to maximise
the well-being of members of society.

Our sale of the widget is almost paradigmatic of the exchanges contemplated in neoclassical economics: it is instant-
aneous; the relationship between the parties does not extend
beyond (or before) the instant of exchange; each party gets

what he expected; bargaining is cooperative and consumes no resources. (In fact, no bargaining is required because market price is known.)

Now, let a widget be a complex thing that takes six months to construct involving a number of components, which are costly to construct as they must be custom-built. There is no ready 'spot' market for them. A can make widgets (or at least convinces B that he can). B thinks he will need a widget in six months' time. If all goes according to plan, having a widget makes B better off by more than it costs A to produce it. A price lying somewhere between these two values will make both parties better off.

The question remains however of finding a means by which each can rely on the other to deliver his part of the bargain: A the widget; B the consideration. Much can happen between now and the delivery date to frustrate the transaction: A could find someone else who wants a widget and is willing to pay more than B; B might find a cheaper source of widgets. The cost of inputs might rise so that making the widget becomes unprofitable. Does A clearly understand that B wants a widget? Does B clearly understand that A is going to supply him with one, etc.?

Clearly, more certainty can be obtained by a formal document which sets out in unambiguous terms the understanding reached between the parties: i.e. a contract. Such a document could also set out the limits to their responsibilities or obligations, e.g. that before B pays he has the right to test whether or not the widget works: that if the wholesale price of widget flanges rise by more than 10 per cent, the contract price should rise by 2 per cent etc. In other words, the contract can provide for certain contingencies and specify who bears the cost *if* they arise – who bears what risks under the contract.

Taking account of all possible occurrences and negotiating who should bear the risk gives rise to transaction costs which, especially in the simplest cases, might more than account for the differences in the value of the widget between the parties. In complex cases not all contingencies might be specified and problems still arise.

Transactions will be facilitated where there exists a body of traditions, conventions or laws which are known by all relevant parties to apply to such transactions. The parties need not spend time and resources deciding on how to deal with contingencies if there already exists a suitable set of rules. Thus transactions are facilitated by the existence of contract law. Similarly, even if certain contingencies are not anticipated by the parties the possibility of their occurring does not burden the transaction because contract law could provide the missing contract clauses, again reducing transaction costs. Contract law supplies many 'implied terms' for contracts.

Thus an established law of contract can be seen as a transaction cost-minimising mechanism. Notice, also, that if the parties do not like how contract law would handle a specific contingency they are at liberty to draw up their own agreement governing that contingency. Contract law does not shackle the parties so long as freedom of contract is the ruling doctrine. This has led Posner (among others) to claim that contract law (and other areas of the common law) are subject to a competitive process. If a certain doctrine is not adequate to the requirement of the parties they will replace it with specific contract terms which are. Over time outdated doctrines will waste away from non-use. If transactions are valued because they increase the welfare of the parties concerned then it will only be welfare-maximising doctrines that survive and contract law will be seen to maximise welfare.

OPTIMAL PROMISES

Because contract law provides sanctions against those that break contracts it will encourage people to be certain they wish to be bound before they enter into them. It will help to minimise the number of non-value-maximising transactions which take place. Thus contract law can be seen as ensuring that the optimal number of contracts are entered into. Goetz and Scott (1980) argue that this can only be obtained when the promisor's decision to make a promise is influenced by the effect which it has on the promisee, i.e. the external effect of the decision to promise must be internalised. This can be done for a non-reciprocal promise by requiring that the promisor pay damages if he defaults. But the damage payment must reflect also the benefits which the promisor receives when he performs.

If the promisor has an idea of the subjective probability that he will perform (p) then his evaluation of the expected value of the promise to the promisee is:

$$pB - (1-p)R$$

where B = the beneficial reliance, and R = detrimental reliance. The expected social value of the promise can be expressed as the sum of the expected value to the promisor (subscript O) and the promisee (subscript E) is:

$$pB_o - (1-p)R_o + pB_E - (1-p)R_E$$

The marginal socially valuable promise will be one where this expression equals zero, i.e.

$$pB_o - (1-p)R_o = (1-p)R_E - pB_E$$
Expected value to promisor = Expected loss to promisee.

(Notice that this is a Kaldor–Hicks-type rule.)

An efficient contract law would, therefore, require the promisor to take account of the effect on the promisee. This can be done according to Goetz and Scott by making the expected value of damages equal to the loss to the promisee, i.e.

$$(1-p) D = (1-p)R_E - pB_E$$

Thus giving a damage rule which sets damages at

$$D = R_E - \frac{PB_E}{(1-p)D} = (1-p)R_E - pB_E$$

Note that damages are not equal to the promisee's detrimental reliances. There is a deduction related to the promisee's beneficial reliances. This deduction tends to zero as p tends to zero, therefore discouraging promises with a low subjective probability of competition.

If we replace $(1-p)R_E - pB_E$ by $(1-p)D$ in the expression for the value of the promise to society we get $pB_o - (1-p)R_o - (1-p)D$, which is actually the value of the promise to the promisor when he takes account of damages:

$$pB_o - (1-p)(R_o+D)$$

When the promise is kept he gets the projected benefits B_o and the promisee gets R_E, and when it is not he suffers some costs plus the damage payment. The expected value of the promise to the promisee is now the expected value to society. (The requirement for compensation does convert it to a Pareto-based rule.)

This formulation does not, however, guarantee that all socially beneficial promises are made, because when $pB_E > (1-p)R_E$, $(1-p)D$ should be negative, i.e. the promisor should be rewarded for making the promise so that even when $pB_o < (1-p)R_o$, i.e. the promisor is made worse off but the promisee is potentially made better off, it is socially desirable that the promise be made. This is impossible for a *non-reciprocal* promise.

The Goetz and Scott optimal damage formula only applies in a way that discourages inefficient promises, it does not ensure that all socially desirable promises are made. This is the key to understanding the basis for such a rule: it is Pareto-based and not Kaldor–Hicks-based, i.e. non-reciprocal promises which have a negative expected value to the promisee should be discouraged because they potentially make the promisee worse off.

Goetz and Scott then go on to argue that things change in a reciprocal contract. In such circumstances the opportunity cost of entering one contract is the benefit forgone of another. In a market setting the opportunity cost is likely to be close to the beneficial reliance, therefore $B_E \approx 0$. Whilst on the other hand, detrimental reliance is likely to be close to full performance. Thus full performance or expectation damages are appropriate. Furthermore, the more reliable a promise is the higher the return promise it will evidence, i.e. the more valuable the consideration. A bargained-for contract seems to offer the parties the opportunity to optimise contract terms and let risks fall on the least-cost insurer.

Goetz and Scott are concerned with the optimal amount of promise-making whereas much of the literature on contract is concerned with the decision to breach or not once the contract has been entered into, i.e. the promise has been made.

OPTIMAL BREACH

Even after a contract has been entered into circumstances will arise where one or other party might be put in a position where completing the contract puts him in a worse position than going through with it.

Posner (1977) focuses on the social efficiency of completing an unwanted contract. If, say, A contracts to buy goods from B at a price P_1 on a certain date and after the contract is entered into B discovers that his materials costs rise dramatically, he may wish to get out of the contract because it costs more to complete than it's worth to him. Posner suggests that it would be a misuse of resources to force completion of the contract: it is no longer value-maximising. However, to ensure that only inefficient contracts are breached the breaching party should compensate the breached-against party in terms of his lost profits.

Let us say that the contract involved B selling to A, at a price p_1, the goods which he thought he could produce at a cost of c_1. A would use them as an input in a good which he would sell at price p_2. (Assume a one-to-one correspondence between units of the two goods.) The value to society of this arrangement is the total profit π, where:

$$\pi = p_2 - p_1 + p_1 - c_1 = p_2 - c_1$$

Assume the cost of one of B's inputs rises uncontrollably to $c_2 > p_1$ making it a loss-maker for him. The social value of the transaction now falls to $p_2 - c_2$. It may no longer be justifiable to commit resources to it. But can we be sure?

An incentive to complete the contract, if it were still socially desirable, would be to require that the breaching party pay damages equal to the breached against party's profits, $p_2 - p_1$. Thus it would only be rational to breach if

$$c_2 - p_1 > p_2 - p_1$$

i.e. $c_2 > p_2$

which implies a negative social value to completing the contract.

As well as providing an incentive to complete socially advantageous contracts this damage rule protects the breached-against party's expectations, i.e. he is not made worse off by the breach. Thus this expectation damage rule would seem to satisfy two desirable objectives: *expectation protection* and *incentive maintenance.*

Notice that we could have obtained the same result by considering whether a fully integrated producer would have gone ahead. In that case private incentives would produce the same result because the integrated producer's profit function would be the same as the joint profit function of the separate producers.

In the previous example expectation damages were set at the breached-against party's profits. Courts will, however, set limits on consequential damages. Failure to complete a contract may endanger a further set of contracts or perhaps a whole business (see *Hadley* v. *Baxendale* [9 Exch 341 (1854)] where a railroad lost a mill-shaft but the court ruled that a valid claim only exists for unforeseeable losses if plaintiff is warned of dangers, indicating some elements of least-cost avoider principle – an extra shaft could be purchased.) The damages may be far in excess of the value of the contract itself. We should also add that the law does not usually require specific performance – that would be wasteful in the case of an efficient breach. We shall look further at specific performances later.

As Barton (1972) (and others) point out the problem is not always as simple as the earlier example because it may be difficult to assess the expectation damages if no market exists for the goods which are the subject of the contract (e.g. custom-made goods). Both parties may have incurred costs which are irretrievable if the contract fails to go through. Parties should be required to mitigate these losses.

We now turn to the question of what sort of damage remedy is required to ensure that contracts which it would be efficient to complete are completed (i.e. only efficient breaches occur). This is a more general treatment than Barton's but not as rigorous as Shavell's (1980).

Let us consider a two-stage process where costs are incurred to produce a good and then further costs are incurred to make it saleable (e.g. packaging or storage). Consider first where the two stages are integrated in one firm. Let the costs of producing the good be c, the costs of making it saleable r, and the price at which it sells S_c. Let the costs incurred at any point before sale be indicated by the subscript i. At any point i the firm may face a decision whether or not to complete the process. If it completes its profits will be given by:

$$\pi^c = S_c - (r_i + r_c) - (c_i + c_c) \text{ per unit.}$$

If it decides not to go ahead its profits are

$$\pi^D = -r_i - c_i$$

(these are its sunk costs).
The firm will decide to abort production if:

$$\pi^D > \pi^C$$
i.e. $-r_i - c_i > S_c - r_i - r_c - c_i - c_c$
i.e. $c_c + r_c - S_c > 0$

i.e. Breach is efficient if the costs of completion exceed the selling price.

Now, consider a situation where there are two firms: a manufacturer (m) who produces the good and an entrepreneur (e) who sells the good and bears the cost of making it saleable. The two firms are linked by a contract which provides for e to pay m at price p per unit. Thus there are two parties who at any point in time i might decide to breach the contract. Let us consider the situation where the entrepreneur is due to pay the price p per unit. He may wish to consider whether to pay the contract price or breach. If the contract goes through the profits of the parties are:

$$\pi_m^c = p - c_i - c_c; \; \pi_e^c = S_c - p - (r_i + r_c)$$
$$\pi_m^b = -c_i; \; \pi_e^b = -r_i.$$

However, contract law will provide a remedy awarding damages against the breaching party. When damages are taken into account the manufacturer's profits become:

$$\pi_m^d = \pi_m^b + d = d - c_i$$

The entrepreneur's profits if he completes are:

$$\pi_e^c = S_c - p - (r_i + r_c)$$

If he breaches they are:

$$\pi_e^d = -r_i - d$$

The entrepreneur will be willing to breach the contract if and only if:

$$\pi^d > \pi_e^c$$

i.e. $-r_i - d > S_c - p - r_i - r_c$

therefore $-d > S_c - p - r_c$, or $r_c - S_c > d - p$.

Compare this with the decision to complete for the integrated firm:

$$c_c - r_c - S_c > 0.$$

It has been argued that breach is only efficient if a fully integrated firm would decide not to complete. An efficient damage rule will be one that makes the two situations the same.

In principle there are three concepts of damage for breach of contract:

(i) *Expectation damages*: The breached-against party should be put in the position he would have been in were the contract completed.
(ii) *Reliance damages*: The breached-against party should be compensated for any reliance expenditures.
(iii) *Restitution damages*: The breaching party returns to the breached against party all payments made to him.

In our example of breach by the entrepreneur no payments were made to him therefore (iii) is, for the moment, irrelevant. Under expectation damages when the entrepreneur breaches damages paid to the manufacturer should be such that:

$$\pi_m^d = \pi_m^c$$

therefore $d - \phi_i = p - \phi_i - c_c$

therefore $d = p - c_c$

therefore $r_c - S_c > p - c_c - p$ for breach

i.e. $r_c + c_c - S_c > 0$, which is the efficient condition

(Note that if all the costs of completion have been incurred $d=p$).

Thus the condition to be met if the entrepreneur is to decide to breach the contract is the same under an expectation damages rule as when the two stages are fully integrated. Thus the expectation damage rule will only lead to breach of contract where breach is efficient.

If the rule for assessing damages in breach of contract is the reliance measure then damages, d, are equal to the reliance expenditures made by the manufacturer which up to point i are c_i, therefore $d = c_i$ which must be less than $p - C_c$ since for π_m to be $> 0; p - C_c > c_i$, therefore damages under the reliance rule are less than under expectation and more breaches will occur (i.e. the reliance rule leads to inefficient breaches occurring).

Let us now consider the case of the manufacturer considering whether or not to breach, at a point in time i, after having received payment, p.

Here

$$\pi_m^c = p - c_c \qquad \pi_e^c = S_c - p - (r_i + r_c)$$
$$\text{and } \pi_m^b = p - c_i \qquad \pi_e^b = r_i - p$$
$$\pi_m^d = -d + p - c_i$$

He will breach if:

$$\pi_m^d > \pi_m^c$$

i.e. $-d + p - c_i > p - v_i - c_c$
$\therefore c_c - d > 0$.

Under an expectation rule, now:

$$d = \pi_e^c - \pi_e^d$$
$$= S_c - r_c$$
$$\therefore c_c + r_c - S_c > 0$$

i.e. the expectation rule is efficient.
Under the reliance measure:

$$d = r_i + p$$

which must be less than $S_c - r_c$ therefore damages are lower for a reliance measure implying that there will be more breaches. Thus under the reliance measure therefore inefficient breaches occur.

Under a restitution measure the manufacturer must return payments made by the entrepreneur,

i.e. $d = p > r_i + p$ which implies $d > S_c - r_c$, therefore inefficient breaches occur.

Consider the following numerical example. Let the selling price (S_c) be 100 and the price which the entrepreneur pays the manufacturer (p) be 70. The production costs up to time i (c_i) are 10 and the costs of making saleable incurred (r_i) also be 10. Let the cost of completion for the manufacturer (c_c) be 10 and those of the entrepreneur's costs of completion (r_e^1) rise to 52 due to some unforeseen contingency. Thus we are really considering how the entrepreneur will react to the rise in his costs of completion. Should he breach his contract or should he complete it?

The profits of an integrated producer under these circumstances are:

$$\pi^c = S_c - c_i - c_c - r_i - r_c^1$$
$$= 100 - 30 - 10 - 10 - 52$$
$$= -2$$

However, if the integrated producer abandoned production his profits are:

$$\pi^D = -r_i - c_i = -20$$

Thus in these circumstances an integrated producer would continue to operate in order to minimise his loss.

The criterion for the integrated firm to cease was that:

$$c_c + r_c - S_c > 0$$
$$\text{i.e. } 10 + 52 - 100 > 0$$

which fails, therefore project should go through.

The criterion under expectation damages is the same therefore it would yield completion. We can see this further in that profits to the entrepreneur if he defaults are:

$$\pi_e^d = -d - r_i$$
$$d = p - c_c = 70 - 10 = 69$$

$$\therefore \pi_e^d = -69 - 10 = -79$$

His profits if he completes are:

$$\pi_e^c = S_c - p - (Cr_i + r_c^1)$$
$$= 100 - 79 - 52$$
$$= -41$$

Thus he has an incentive to complete.
If damages are reliance damages they are:

$$d = c_i = 30$$
$$\therefore \pi_e^d = -30 - 10 = -40$$
$$\pi_e^c = -41$$

Therefore the entrepreneur would breach, which is inefficient.
Now consider the case where the manufacturer might breach. Let all the figures be the same for the time of contract but at time i the manufacturer's costs of completion rise to 89.5,

$$\therefore \pi_m^c = 79 - 30 - 89.5 \qquad \pi_e^c = 100 - 79 - 20 = 1$$
$$= -40.5$$
$$\pi_m^c + \pi_e^c = -39.5$$
$$\pi_m^b = 49 \qquad\qquad\qquad \pi_e^b = -10 - 79 = -89$$
$$\pi_m^b + \pi_e^b = -40.$$

Therefore an integrated firm would complete.
The criterion for breach under expectation damages is:

$$c_c + r_c - S_c > 0$$
$$89.5 + 10 - 100 > 0$$
i.e. breach is not efficient

We can see this by looking at the manufacturer's position. If he defaults his profits are $\pi_m^a = -d + p - c_i$ under expectation damages $d = S_c - r_c = 90$

$$\therefore \pi_m^d = -90 + 79 - 30 = -41$$
$$\pi_m^c = -40.5$$

Therefore he will complete.
Under reliance damages $d = r_i + p = 89$

$$\therefore \pi_m^d = -89 + 79 - 30 = -40$$

Therefore he breaches.

Under restitution $d = p = 79$

$$\therefore \pi_m^d = -79 + 79 - 30_i = -30$$

Therefore he breaches.

However we should notice that we have assumed in both problems that reliance expenditures are kept to a minimum. However on all bases for compensation except the restitution measure all reliance is compensated. Thus the breached-against party may incur excessive reliance expenditures. Remember the entrepreneur will breach if $r_c - S_c > d - p$. If the manufacturer has incurred all completion costs

$$d = p$$

Therefore the criterion is $r_c - S_c > 0$, therefore it is less likely that he will breach, i.e. in some cases where breach was efficient it will not take place. This provides an incentive for the manufactuter to spend on completion costs.

Under reliance d will now equal $c_i + c_c$, therefore the criterion becomes:

$$r_c - S_c > c_i + c_c - p$$

instead of $r_c - S_c > c_i - p$. Therefore where breach was efficient it might not be if there is excessive reliance.

In this sub-section we have seen that, given the assumptions of the model, an expectation damages rule will only result in breaches of contract which are efficient. The reliance and restitution rules may result in inefficient breaches taking place. However, only the reliance rule ensures efficient reliance expenditures, therefore the expectation and reliance rules can result in excessive reliance expenditures.

SPECIFIC PERFORMANCE

Thus far, the only class of remedies for breach of contract which we have consider are damage awards. In Chapter 5 the distinction between *property rules* and *liability rules* developed by Calabresi and Melamed (1972) was used to analyse remedies. The distinction was that property rules required the consent of the entitlement holder to the transfer of the entitlement to another whilst under a liability rule the entitlement holder was compensated for the involuntary transfer of the entitlement.

The analogue to a property rule in contract is *specific performance*: the breaching party is required to perform according to the terms of the contract which is the 'entitlement' of the breached-against party. Specific performance is not a widely used remedy. Why should this be? As Ogus and Veljanovski (1984, p. 81) point out, we would expect, if anything, it to be the case. First because contracts are usually between two parties and thus there are not the 'free-rider' or 'hold-out' problems that might accompany the use of a property rule in a nuisance case (and anyway British judges seem to prefer a property rule in the nuisance context). Secondly, the parties to the contract have voluntarily entered into a legal relationship whereas in nuisance or tort cases they have not.

We can identify four arguments against specific performance.

(1) Specific performance cannot handle the doctrines of remoteness and mitigation which are necessary to ensure efficient behaviour by the promisee.

(2) The administrative costs of specific performance are greater than those associated with damages because the court will have to supervise performance whereas damages require no supervision.

(3) A more widely available use of specific performance may increase *pre-breach costs* if the law as it stands does already grant specific performance in all areas where the parties desire it. In areas where the parties did not desire specific performance they would be required to negotiate contract terms which precluded it. This would raise transaction costs (Kronman, 1978).

(4) If promisees were entitled to specific performance, but the cost of specific performance to the promisor exceeded the costs at the time of breach by more than the benefits of specific performance to the promisee exceeded the

latter's 'benefit' under breach, then the promisor should 'bribe' the promisee to waive his right to specific performance: there is a net gain to be allocated between the parties via negotiation. Such negotiation will generate transaction costs which could be avoided by having court imposed damages (Posner, 1977).

Let us examine in more detail the *pre-breach* and *post-breach* costs arguments. As far as the pre-breach costs dimension is concerned, Kronman argues that *specific performance* is in general limited to *unique goods* and it is for this category of goods that parties would voluntarily negotiate a specific performance remedy were there no general rule. A promisor's evaluation of specific performance will depend on the likelihood that he will wish to breach: if that is zero specific performance is not an issue for him and he will be indifferent between specific performance and damages. The promisor will only wish to breach if he is better off by doing so. This requires that the new price offered, say, exceeds the contract price by more than the damage award. Thus the probability must be a function of the probability of such a higher offer materialising. Where this probability is greater than zero the promisor would favour damages; when it is zero he is indifferent. Kronman argues that where the good is unique the probability is low (perhaps zero) therefore the promisor is indifferent between the rules for unique goods. Where it is high he prefers damages.

How does the promisee look at the choice of rule? He is likely to have a non-zero belief that the promisor will breach. The question is one of how well the method of relief will put the promisee in the position he would have been in had the contract been performed. For a unique good with no established market, assessment of its worth to the promisee may be difficult. The question is essentially, 'What is the loss of surplus to the promisee as a result of the breach?' It is likely to be very difficult for a court to assess this in making a damages award and therefore damages may under-compensate the promisee. Thus for unique goods it is argued that the promisee would prefer specific performance.

In the case of non-unique goods it is more easy to establish value, according to Kronman. Therefore, under-compensation is less likely and the promisee is indifferent.

In sum then, Kronman argues that for *unique* goods the promisor is indifferent between remedies whilst the promisee prefers specific performance. Therefore specific performance would be chosen. For *non-unique* goods the promisor prefers damages whilst the promisee is indifferent therefore damages would be chosen. Thus Kronman argues that the restricted availability of specific performance is efficient because it corresponds to what the parties would choose if they were free to negotiate but it avoids the transaction costs involved in the negotiation.

Attiyah (1981b) has criticised Kronman on the grounds that the latter's arguments are conducted in terms of contracts for the sale of chattels, whilst in England, at least, the most common instance of decrees for specific enforcement concern contracts to sell or lease houses or other buildings for which there is an extensive market and (usually) a reasonably ascertainable market price. Attiyah's point, however, is flawed because it is not the absence of the market which is important to Kronman's argument about uniqueness but the difficulty of estimating the loss of surplus to the disappointed promisee. The problem is rather similar to the one raised in Chapter 6 in connection with the fairness of market price compensation for compulsory purchase. Houses are unique; no two share exactly the same characteristics, therefore market price under-estimates the value to the owner (or in this case the promisee). Houses are unique in the sense which Kronman uses the term.

Schwartz (1979) criticises Kronman's analysis on more substantial grounds. He argues that markets for unique goods are likely to be characterised by higher price dispersions than those for non-unique goods. Furthermore, sellers of unique goods face a lower 'rate of arrival' of potential buyers. This is because there is less comparison shopping due to the higher search costs. This implies that the seller of a unique good will regard the offers he receives as random and that later offers may be higher. Therefore he may regard the likelihood of breach to be higher and thus would actually prefer damages to specific performance.

Schwartz further argues that this conclusion is buttressed by a consideration of the effects of exogenous shocks in markets for unique and non-unique goods. In a market for non-unique goods an exogenous shock which increases demand (i.e. shifts the demand curve) will induce an increase in price but the price rise will be dampened by the ability of producers to increase supply. The more elastic demand, the lower the price increase and the less inducement there is for suppliers to breach contracts fixed at the original price (p_1) (see Figure 8.1) The supply of unique goods will be highly inelastic and consequently any shift of the demand curve will bring about a greater increase in price increasing the probability that existing contracts will be breached. (In the unique goods market actual prices are dispersed around the price p_1 and p_2.) Thus, Schwartz argues that, contrary to Kronman's assertion, promisors in unique goods markets have a preference for damages over specific performance. Therefore the use of specific performance in unique goods markets cannot be explained on the basis that it is what the parties would choose if they were free to do so.

The fourth argument against specific performance was that it would increase transaction costs due to post-breach negotiations. Say specific performance were available and a contract provided for A to supply B at a price P_C. There is then an exogenous shock which sends the market into disequilibrium and A receives an offer of $P_D > P_C$; A will wish to breach. Let us say that the market subsequently settles down at P_E where $P_D > P_E > P_C$. B will demand specific performance. He is worse off by $P_E - P_C$ which he could get in damages but by demanding specific performance he forces A to share with him the remaining profit, $P_D - P_E$. Thus specific performance generates increased transactions costs. It is also arguable that damages generate transaction costs. If only a damage remedy is available negotiations may take place prior to going to court since each party can threaten to inflict on the other costs of going to court. The choice between the two depends on which set of transactions costs are the lower. Schwartz accepts that those associated with the damage rule are likely to be smaller since breaching sellers are likely to settle quickly.

However, Schwartz argues that there may be a false assumption here. Why can't A go into the market and purchase at P_E

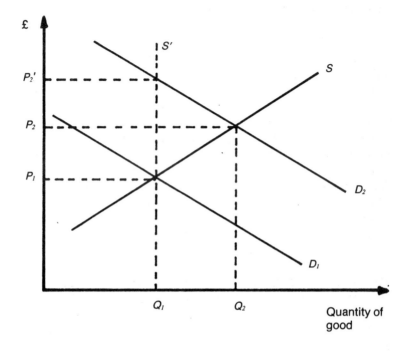

Figure 8.1

and supply to B, thus performing. The only grounds for not doing this would be if B could incur lower transaction costs than A in acquiring at P_E. This seems unlikely. Thus specific performance does *not* necessitate post-breach negotiations in the case of a non-unique good and therefore it does not reduce welfare. Schwartz, therefore, argues that an extension of specific performance would be justified. He further argues that efficiency would be enhanced (as Kronman argued) where there is a risk of under-compensation and hence damages might induce inefficient breaches. It would also remove the need for negotiated liquidated damages clauses or strategic behaviour by promisee's when large liquidated damages are available. In complex cases specific performance may have lower transaction costs than assessing damages.

STANDARD-FORM CONTRACTS

The preceding sections of this chapter have dealt at a very general level with 'contracts'. The implicit presumption, following on from the introductory section, was that these contracts were the result of negotiations between the parties involved. However, very many transactions (if not the majority) in advanced societies are governed by contracts which have not been the subject of such negotiations (Slawson, 1971, p. 259; Attiyah, 1981a, ch. 1). These are *standard-form* contracts drawn up unilaterally by the seller and presented to the buyer on a take-it-or-leave-it basis. They are contracts of adhesion. The standard-form contract pervades all aspects of modern life. The purchase of a ticket to ride a train, bus or aeroplane is the acceptance of a standard-form contract. So too is the acceptance of an insurance policy, a mortgage, a hire purchase agreement, the consuming of gas, electricity, telephone and other utility services. Indeed, acceptance of a place at a university usually involves accepting the rules of the university as laid down in its statutes or similar document which then is the basis of the student's contract with the university. The list is virtually endless. The common feature of all of these contracts is that they involve no negotiation over terms. The terms are standard for all purchases and are set out by the suppliers. Standard-form contracts are not restricted to transactions involving consumers and producers. Many commercial transactions in which both parties are producers (i.e. organisations) are governed by standard contracts. These can vary from conditions of acceptance printed on the back of an order form to detailed provisions negotiated at industry level such as those extensively used in civil engineering.

Judicial (and indeed, legislative) sentiment runs against standard-form contracts. They are liable to be regarded as 'unconscionable' or made under duress. This attitude contrasts with the judiciary's basic sympathy with freedom of contract, i.e. contracts freely entered into by responsible adults should be enforced. The conflict is inherently between nineteenth-century legal principles which are nominally still valid and the realities of the modern commercial world which have led to piecemeal changes in application (Attiyah, 1981a, ch. 1;

MacNeil, 1978). However, the suspicion of standard-form contracts also arises from a view consistent with much neoclassical economics writing which sees monopoly purposes lying behind anything that does not fit the paradigm of exchange between equals (Williamson, 1979; 1985). This is what George Priest (1981), in the context of consumer product warranties, has called the *exploitation theory*; the producer by virtue of market power or collusion with other producers is restricting the choices open to consumers and imposing on them the terms of the 'bargain'. Michael Trebilcock (1980) has used the term 'structurally impaired markets' to describe the circumstances that would give rise to such a use of the standard-form contract. However, the mere existence of a standard-form contract is not evidence of such market failure for other factors (see further below) may be the source. Trebilcock (1980) and Trebilcock and Dewees (1981) argue further that the courts may not be the appropriate forum in which to determine whether there is such structural impairment. That would be a matter, in the first instance at least, for anti-trust or regulatory authorities.

Another potential source of the anti-social use of standard-form contracts arises from what Trebilcock (1980) calls *informationally impaired markets*. Here there are informational asymmetries whereby one party is unaware (or cannot know) what other terms (more advantageous to him) are available elsewhere, or that the terms offered are disadvantageous to him. It is perhaps, reasonable to assume that such circumstances are more likely to arise in the case of producer/consumer contracts than for producer/producer contracts. This may account for the disposition of courts to accept more readily standard-form contracts in the latter circumstances than in the former.

On the other hand, standard-form contracts may actually serve an efficiency-enhancing role: they reduce transaction costs. For example, consider the purchase of a ticket to a cinema or theatre or a rail ticket. These are all forms of unilateral standard-form contracts. The purchaser agrees to the terms laid down by the supplier often without even having seen them. What would happen if every commuter sought to negotiate an individual contract each time he travelled? The real cost of travel would rise astronomically for both parties. The standard-form contract economises on transaction costs in this instance.

The reader should be wary, however, of concluding from this that whatever terms happen to be offered by the rail operator are efficient. All that is being said is that individual negotiations would be inefficient. Some other mechanism for aggregating preferences of consumers and reconciling these with the economics of the undertaking will require to be found. In the case of a public utility such as rail transport, competition does not provide a solution because of a strong element of natural monopoly. In other areas, however, competition between suppliers on the terms on which the good or service is offered might reduce inefficiency even if standard terms are offered to each consumer by a given competing supplier. So long as entry by new suppliers was feasible any supplier offering 'unfair' terms risks attracting new suppliers into the market by the super-normal profits which it earns. Brand loyalty and product differentiation might mean that the price/terms combination on offer could remain above the competitive package in the long run. This might lead to excess capacity as predicted by the theory of monopolistic competition. This is inefficient in conventional terms, but as Chamberlin (1933) argued, consumers might well value the 'choice' which this permits.

In this context it is worth noting that in a perfectly competitive environment all firms would be offering the same competitive terms. Thus the fact that all firms in a market offer the same contractual terms is not evidence of structural impairment. The existence of super-normal profits or excessive costs would also need to exist.

On the other hand, potential entrants only exert a restraining influence on firms in an industry where a market is 'contestable'. If there are economies of scale in the industry entry is only feasible at the minimum efficient scale. Thus, a price and terms variant of a limit pricing strategy could be used to deter entry at the same time as sustaining supernormal profits (see Waterson, 1984, ch. 4). Evaluating these considerations would not seem to be the forte of common law judges.

Standard terms may also be sustained if consumers are unwilling to incur the search costs associated with finding a supplier who will trade on better terms. This, of course, is another way of minimising transaction costs. It can be rational and efficient. However, the doctrine of unconscionability could give rise to the consumer 'having his cake and eating it' if he accepts the standard terms (to reduce transaction costs) and then has them declared unconscionable. It might be more effective to have a 'cooling-off period' during which the purchaser can revoke the contract. Such provisions exist in the UK in the case of hire purchase and other financial contracts.

The import of much of the argument set out here is that the doctrine of unconscionability must be situationally sensitive. The courts must go beyond the terms of the contract and examine the social and economic context in which it is embedded. The failure of courts (and legislators) to do this can give rise to results which from the economist's perspective are, at least, questionable.

Consider the case of *Macauley* v. *Schroeder Publishing Co. Ltd* ([1970] 1 WLR 1308 HL) concerning a contract between a composer and a music publisher. (A more detailed discussion of the case is provided in Trebilcock (1980) and Trebilcock and Dewees (1981).) The facts of the case are that an unknown songwriter contracted with a publisher, using a standard form, to assign the copyright to all his songwriting output for a term of five years to the publisher in exchange for £50 and 50 per cent of all net royalties in songs actually published. The publisher had a right, on certain conditions, to exercise an option to extend the contract for a further five years, to terminate the contract on one month's notice, and to assign the copyright without the composer's permission. On the other hand, the composer had no right to terminate and could only assign the agreement with the publisher's consent. The House of Lords upheld the Appeal Court's unanimous judgment that the contract was unenforceable. Both courts concluded that the contract imposed unreasonable restraints on the ability of the composer to market his services. In the judgment in the House of Lords, Lord Diplock pointed out that the publisher's bargaining power *vis-à-vis* the composer required special vigilance on the part of the court to ensure that it has not used it. As Trebilcock and Dewees (1981, p. 99) conclude: 'the fact that the court struck down the contract means, of course, in the court's view ... superior bargaining power had in fact been abused.'

There is no suggestion, however, that the music publishing market is monopolised or that the composer was not aware of the existence of other publishers. What is relevant to the nature of the contract is that at the contract stage the publisher is not able to distinguish a potential hit songwriter from any other unknown songwriter. A publisher will be offered many hundreds, if not thousands, of songs every year, few of which will be money-makers and most of which will not merit publishing. Thus the publisher incurs costs in a highly uncertain environment: much of the income from successful songs being used as signing-on payments to the unsuccessful writers. What is important here is the entire business of the publishers, not just the profitable section of its portfolio of investments. If a songwriter had freedom to contract with any publisher for each of his songs then clearly once he was a 'success' he could sell to the highest bidder leaving the publisher of his prior unsuccessful songs having incurred losses. As Trebilcock and Dewees point out, the consequence of this might be that no publisher would be willing to 'invest' in unknown composers who might find themselves having to pay publishers to publish their songs until they had a success. What the courts' judgments are doing is attempting to reallocate the risks (and costs) of publishing. Such a reallocation would not leave other dimensions of the relationship between writers and publishers undisturbed: they will adjust to reflect the new distribution of risks and costs.

Another example where a standard form of contract contains terms which courts may view as evidence of unequal bargaining power is the use of 'add-on' clauses in consumer contracts (Epstein, 1975). These clauses deal with the question of security for credit terms. It is not uncommon, particularly in the United States, for a credit contract to be secured not only on the item for which credit is sought but on all other goods still subject to a similar contract between the parties. For example A buys a refrigerator from B on credit terms extending over two years. One year into this contract A buys a

stereo from B on similar terms except that the contract for the
stereo is 'added on' to the contract for the refrigerator. After a
further ten months A defaults on payment for the stereo and
by the terms of contract B repossesses both the stereo *and* the
refrigerator even though the payments on the latter are almost
complete and may even be continuing to be met.

Some US courts, at least, would seem to take the view that
such a credit arrangement, arising from the use of standard
terms, results from an inequality of bargaining power. This is
frequently evidenced by the fact that the consumers concerned
will be on low incomes, poorly educated, from minority
groups, living in poor quality, rented accommodation, whilst
the seller is a profitable corporation or store. In extreme cases
payments for previously purchased items may be consolidated
with new payments for the new items and apportioned *pro rata*
so that the earlier contracts are never discharged so long as
new goods are being purchased. Consequently, default on payments may result in the repossession of goods purchased
several years ago and the purchase price of which is only a
fraction of payments already made to the seller. (This, of
course, also raises the question of the penalty for breach of
contract exceeding the value of the contract itself.) Epstein
(1975) argues that such 'add-on' clauses may be seen as being
in the interests of the consumer as well as the vendor. The
consumers who use such contracts are typically those with
little other security to offer for a credit contract and the items
covered (stereos, for example) may often be easily damaged
and have low resale value after repossession. Therefore, on
repossession the item which is the subject of the contract will
have a value below that of the debt so that repossession of that
item is not a credible sanction on the purchaser who has few
owned assets. The only assets are those previously purchased
on credit. Furthermore, if a continuing credit relationship is
developed, perhaps because the vendor is located in the
community in which the purchaser lives, the sanction against a
defaulter becomes credible. Remove such a credit arrangement
and the purchaser may not be able to secure credit terms
because he is a high risk. Thus, this arrangement may be to the
advantage of the purchaser. What is *prima facie* an inequitable
contract is, when viewed from a relational contract perspective

(see further below), actually in the interests of the purchaser (or the class of purchasers of which the actual purchaser is a member). However, it should be clearly understood that this is not unambiguously the case. The contract has to be viewed in the circumstances in which it is made in order to determine whose interests it serves. The courts must be situationally sensitive.

A very common standard-form contract is the consumer product warranty. The warranty delimits the expectations of the consumer which the supplier undertakes to make good. Since they are expressed terms of the contract they, therefore, make clear the intentions of the parties. However, since the warranty is frequently in standard form, drawn up by the supplier and presented to the purchaser on a take-it-or-leave-it basis, it is subject to the same judicial suspicion as any other standard-form contract. As mentioned above, the 'exploitation theory' has been implicit in much of the judicial and legislative treatment of consumer product warranties. A brief review of the origins and consequences of the exploitation theory is given in Priest (1981, pp. 1299–302). Promoters of the exploitation theory argue that standard-form warranties may be used by producers to escape the implied warranty of merchantability and to protect the producer against the consequences of misleading or dishonest advertising. There would seem to be considerable evidence for the exploitation theory in the numbers of cases on which vendors sought to defend themselves by recourse to warranty provisions which the courts deemed exploitative.

A leading American case which has been followed in almost all US jurisdictions is *Henningsen* v. *Bloomfield Motors Inc.* (32 N.J. 358, 408, 161 A 2d 69, 97 [1960]) which concerns serious personal injury from an alleged product defect. In this case the warranty disclaimed the implied warranty of merchantability, excluded consequential damage and limited warranty to repair or replacement of the defective part. The New Jersey Supreme Court refused to enforce the terms of the warranty on grounds which are consistent with the exploitation theory.

In recent years a literature has been developing on the economics of the market for information. This derives from a recognition that the acquisition of information involves costs and that it will be rational for economic agents to seek to reduce these costs where feasible. A major category of information costs is search costs. Efficiency will be enhanced by any mechanism which reduces, *ceteris paribus*, such costs. Thus informative advertising by producers reduces the costs which otherwise would be incurred by consumers in finding and comparing alternative brands of a desired product. Seen in this light search costs are, of course, an *ex ante* transaction cost. The producer can 'signal' information about his product in a number of ways: its price, ancillary services, the nature of his sales premises, and the nature of the warranty which he provides with its sale. Although this specialist literature is of relatively recent origin, usually dated from the seminal paper by George Stigler (1961), it has antecedents in notions of product differentiation (Chamberlin, 1933) and the notion of markets in general, and prices in particular, as information-transmitting systems (Hayek, 1945).

A proposition has developed that standard-form warranties are a means by which producers can send signals to consumers about the quality and reliability of their products (Gerner and Bryant, 1978; 1981). Priest (1981) refers to this as the *market signal theory of warranty*. If a producer has invested a great deal of time, money and effort to make his product reliable in all sorts of conditions he has an incentive to 'signal' this to potential consumers of the product, by guaranteeing its reliability in these conditions (or at least not excluding them from the general terms of the warranty). Conversely a producer who has not made such an investment is likely to embody such exclusions in the warranty. Thus the consumer can deduce from the terms of the producer's warranty the reliability of that particular brand. An interesting facet of this view is that, if it holds, consumers require no technical knowledge to evaluate the reliability of a product *ex ante*. The consumer can rely on the extensiveness of the producer's warranty as an indicator of the product's reliability. Consumers will, of course, still make mistakes but under the market signal theory these mistakes arise from the costs and benefits of using the warranty as an information processing tool.

Three major implications have been derived from the signal

theory (Gerner and Bryant, 1981; Priest, 1981):

(i) Warranties for different products will contain similar, if not identical, provisions.
(ii) Where warranty provisions diverge from standard provisions they will be more generous.
(iii) Subordinate terms are more likely to diverge from standard terms and to be restrictive.

The first implication arises because the purchase of a specific consumer durable is an infrequent occurrence and it is consumer durables that are most widely sold with a warranty. Consumers will not be in the market for a TV (for example) very frequently. Thus if warranties carried a great deal of information specific to the reliability of one particular appliance the consumer would not have much of a basis on which to evaluate the warranty's significance or reliability. However, consumers in western industrialised economies do own large numbers of consumer durables and are likely to be frequently in the market for one type or another. Therefore, if warranty terms are similar for TVs, fridges, cars, cookers, stereos, etc., the consumer can infer that one product will be as reliable as another with the same warranty of which he has had experience. The consumer may then be attracted to those brands of a particular durable which have general terms rather than product-specific terms.

The implication concerning the direction of deviation from the standard terms is derived from an assumption that consumers will, in fact, assume that a specific good offers the same warranty terms as the average or typical warranty. Consequently, if the product suffers a defect the consumer will assume that it is covered by warranty if such a defect is generally covered. Thus he will make a claim which will impose costs on the producer because the claim will have to be processed. If a producer produces a product which is less reliable than the average even where he 'signals' this by offering a below-average warranty he will still have to process claims because consumers will not 'pick up the signal'. Therefore it is not rational to produce warranties with below-average terms because this will give rise to administrative costs and a loss of goodwill of customers who expect average terms.

Consequently, the only rational deviations from average warranty terms will be where the warranty provides 'above average' protection to the consumer.

On the other hand, it is argued that consumers are unlikely to be aware of the details of subordinate provisions in warranties (frequently relating to exclusions and limitations of coverage). Thus consumers are unlikely to have expectations about the content of such clauses and to make claims based on these false expectations. Therefore, there will be fewer claims and, in particular, fewer invalid claims. The producer will therefore be freer to set warranty terms with reference to the cost of coverage. Furthermore, because of consumer ignorance there will be less competitive pressure to offer the average in the case of subordinate terms. Note that with respect to subordinate terms the signal and exploitation theories converge.

A study by Gerner and Bryant (1981) of the content of 180 warranties covering various consumer durables finds a degree of support for the implications of the signal theory. Most warranties provide coverage of parts and labour costs for one year. However, those which deviate from this tend to be more limiting rather than more extensive, as the theory would seem to predict. Subsidiary clauses are found to be more hetero-geneous and related to the producer's costs.

George Priest (1981) has developed an *investment theory of warranty* which embodies the least-cost avoider principle. He characterises a warranty as providing two services: insurance and repairs. In principle, either the producer or consumer could undertake these. The transaction costs of allocating responsibility for these in a particular case can be reduced by having a standard warranty contract providing for their allocation between parties. In a transaction cost-free world cooperative bargaining would result in the distribution of these responsibilities in a least-cost manner.

What are the respective costs of the producer and the consumer in providing the insurance service? The producer would have to cover the losses that occur plus the cost of aggregating the claims (known technically as the *loading cost*). This additional cost of providing the insurance cover will be incorporated in the price of the product. Alternatively the consumer could self-insure by, for example, saving a certain sum every period to provide the means to replace the defective product. The consumer would also have to bear transaction costs under such a strategy. Thus the warranty would be provided by the producer if the sum of the expected loss plus loading costs was less than the sum of the expected loss plus transaction costs.

Similarly repair costs will be covered by the warranty if the producer can provide them more cheaply than the consumer. This will depend on the nature of the defect: some may be more cheaply repaired by the manufacturer, some by the consumer. However, repair costs can also be reduced, *ceteris paribus*, by consumers taking more care when using the product or by the manufacturer designing the product in a way which safeguards against damage. Both of these are allocative investments designed to increase the life of the product by altering the probability of defect whilst self-insurance and market insurance deal with the allocation of the burden of dealing with a defect once it occurs. It is obvious that these are substitutes for each other. Priest argues that which of them is chosen will be determined by the least-cost principle. In his view, a warranty 'is the instrument that expresses consumer preferences for allocative or insurance investments. It is a contract that divides responsibility for allocative investments and insurance between the consumer and the manufacture. The content of the contract is determined by the respective costs to the two parties of allocative investments or insurance' (Priest, 1981, p. 1313). Priest, therefore, suggests that the investment theory of warranties predicts that disclaimers of liability and exclusions of coverage will be observed for those allocative or insurance investments which the consumer can provide more cheaply than the manufacturer.

Priest (1981) examines the explanatory power of the three theories of warranty by examining the provisions of 62 warranties covering 16 product groups. He concludes that the predictions of the investment theory seem to be more consistent with the evidence than those of the other theories. However, he does caution that this might be a consequence of that theory being based on a more easily measured concept (costs) than either the exploitation theory (market power) or the signal theory (information costs). Secondly, aspects of design, manufacture and use of a product are more likely to be determined by costs than market power or consumer information. Thus the investment theory is a more general theory (and therefore is richer in its implications) than the other theories.

NEO-INSTITUTIONALISM

The final part of this chapter on contract turns to an approach sometimes referred to as relational contracting, sometimes transaction cost economics, and sometimes neo-institutional economics. The use of the term 'transaction cost economics' is not very helpful in the context of this book because it is almost all about transaction costs. However transaction costs thus far have been viewed as a sort of friction in the market exchange system which would lead us to prefer one set of rules for settling a dispute to others.

The focus of the analysis has been on how society through the 'law' and the courts resolves disputes between two units seeking to maximise their own benefit. This is done by choosing rules that result in the benefit to society being maximised. Transaction costs are taken as given.

The approach discussed in this section focuses on transaction costs and by analysing what causes them seeks to examine the way that maximising units will organise themselves so as to minimise transaction costs. This is why it is sometimes referred to as neo-institutional economics: it is concerned with what determines the structure of economic institutions not how existing institutions behave. In a sense this approach is much older than 'law-and-economics'. It has antecedents in American institutional economics which was in its heyday from the turn of the century to the mid-1930s. Neo-institutionalism is more directly traceable to a paper published by Ronald Coase in 1937 (*The Nature of the Firm*). These two traditions lay dormant till the 1970s when they were combined with some of the ideas of Herbert Simon and the Carnegie School by Oliver Williamson particularly in his book *Markets and Hierarchies*.

Williamson's approach has many applications but its central

focus is on how a transaction or exchange will be mediated: How is it governed – by a market exchange? by an administrative decision within an organisation? by some form of quasi-integration? In a sense Williamson's approach might be best seen as trying to answer the question: Why are some transactions not handled by a market exchange while others are? Williamson's answer is that the costs of using the market are too high in some cases. What are the costs of using the market? They are the costs of finding someone to contract with, reaching an agreement, monitoring and policing it (i.e. transaction costs). This gives rise to the next question: What is it that makes these costs differ between situations? It is the posing of this question that is Williamson's fundamental contribution to economics.

Williamson (1975; 1979; 1985) argues that two sets of factors are important in determining transaction costs: (i) human characteristics, and (ii) environmental characteristics. The first human characteristic is *bounded rationality*. Human behaviour is 'intendedly rational but only limitedly so', to use Simon's phrase. Much economic theory treats human beings as hyper-rational. Bounds are set on our rationality by the computational (neurophysiological) limits of our brains and by language limitations – our inability to convey completely our thoughts to others. The second human characteristic is *opportunism*. Economists usually analyse behaviour on the assumption that humans are self-interested – they maximise utility. Opportunism extends this to self-seeking with *guile*. An analogy with the old distinction in cricket between gentlemen and players might be useful here (gentlemen are amateurs; players, professionals). The usual economic agent is assumed to be a gentleman he plays by the book, is truthful and never behaves strategically. The opportunistic economic agent will use any ploy available to gain a strategic advantage in bargaining: he uses threats; he holds back information; he will take advantage of his adversary's ignorance. Williamson does not suggest that all economic agents behave opportunistically only that some do, but it is costly to sort out who are who in advance.

These human characteristics are not sufficient on their own to generate transaction costs. It is only when they are paired with certain environmental characteristics that they do. The first environmental characteristic is *uncertainty/complexity.* Bounded rationality is not a problem with simple situations or determinate situations. If all possible outcomes are known with certainty and there are not many it may be easy to draw up a fully comprehensive *contingent claims contract* – one that says what the obligations of the parties will be in all possible states. Very often, however, even if a problem is determinate it is complex (e.g. chess). Most importantly for contractual relations, the world is uncertain. We cannot predict all contingencies. Thus the pairing of bounded rationality with complexity/uncertainty can generate transaction costs – difficulties in drawing up a contingent claims contract.

However, the pairing of bounded rationality with uncertainty/ complexity would not be a problem but for *opportunism.* In the absence of opportunism all contracts could include a clause by which each party undertook to act in all circumstances in the best interests of the parties jointly. Thus gaps in the contract would not be exploited to the advantage of one party and the detriment of the other. No party would exploit any asymmetric knowledge which was available on the true state of the contract (no information impactedness).

The second environmental characteristic of relevance is what Williamson calls the *small numbers condition.* Opportunism is not really a problem where a transaction (or contract) is of a recurring nature: if a party behaves opportunistically on one occasion he is unlikely to be awarded the contract on an other occasion. Thus frequency of transaction is of importance. A second dimension of the small numbers condition is the number of potential suppliers (or customers). The larger this number the more competitive will be the process by which contract terms are arrived at. Part of the competitive process will be the willingness of parties to reveal information to which the other party does not have access. Thus the larger the number of potential suppliers the less likely *ex ante* opportunistic behaviour will be to arise.

Opportunistic behaviour might still arise *ex post* due to information impactedness or to *first mover advantage* – the fact that the party successful on the first round may have a strategic advantage in negotiations for subsequent contracts. A large numbers situation is effectively converted into a small numbers situation in subsequent rounds (e.g. local TV and radio franchises). The pairing of the small numbers condition with opportunism gives rise to transactions costs. The pairings of human characteristics and environmental conditions can be shown schematically thus:

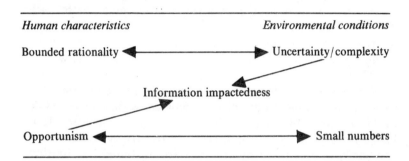

A final concept used by Williamson is what he calls *atmosphere*; the overall conditions within which the transaction takes place. This may be of utility to the parties by itself (e.g. cooperativeness/individuality): e.g. in Japan transactions are usually made in an atmosphere of mutual respect and cooperativeness – opportunistic behaviour would be subject to social sanction. In the US with its individualistic ethic opportunistic behaviour is expected – indeed, it may be the norm.

Williamson initially developed his theory to explain the phenomenon of vertical integration between sequential stages of a production process. Why was the transaction between the two technologically independent stages not mediated by the market? Conventional theory has seen this as anti-competitive but you need very special conditions for this. Williamson argued that often it might be in order to minimise transaction costs. He went on to demonstrate that this framework could be applied to various situations to explain why particular economic institutions arise – internal labour markets, franchising, the multi-divisional firm. For the present purpose we are interested in what the approach tells us about contractual relations.

Williamson talks about 'minimising' transaction costs in the same way that we might talk about minimising production costs – as though there were an explicit cost function to be minimised. This preserves a neoclassical optimising framework. Victor Goldberg (1984) has suggested that this gives rather the wrong impression. He prefers to talk of transactional *difficulties* rather than costs. Agents will avoid those ways of mediating transactions which give rise to such difficulties or have a potential for them to arise. Goldberg's approach gives the flavour of strategic decision-making which seems appropriate but the more generally used terms will be used here.

Williamson's framework was essentially developed to explain why some transactions occurred within firms while others occur between firms (i.e. hierarchy vs. market). It is based on a paradigm of contract – those transactions which can easily be governed by contract are mediated by contract whilst those that cannot usually take place within a firm. The markets/hierarchies framework is too simplistic, however. There are many quasi-market or quasi-integrated ways of governing transactions. Williamson's framework is also useful in identifying these.

A number of scholars have pointed out that contracts often take a form very different from the classical notion of a discrete exchange. Many contracts foresee a continuing relationship between the parties. They are relational contracts. Williamson's framework can be used to identify the circumstances under which relational contracts will arise.

Much of Williamson's work has focused on the *small numbers condition*. Notice that the human characteristics of bounded rationality and opportunism are always potentially present. Simple environments pose little problem whilst uncertainty is almost always with us. We have seen that the small numbers condition involves both the frequency with which the transaction is likely to occur and the number of potential contractors. The latter is likely to be related to how specialised the transaction is: are there costs that must be incurred to support the transaction but which cannot be covered if the transaction falls through? Such costs Williamson calls *transaction-specific investment*. They are investments because they are incurred now on the expectation that they will generate benefits in the future (i.e. the benefits of the transaction). But the investment is specific to the transaction. Williamson refers to such a situation as *idiosyncratic exchange*. However, it is likely that the situation will not be black-and-white. There may be degrees of specificity of investment supporting the transaction. It may have a limited number of alternative uses rather than none.

It might be helpful in elucidating these concepts if we take a specific example. Consider a firm deciding to set up a car assembly plant in a country where there have been no locally-produced cars. Amongst other things the firm will need a supply of body shells and panels. These are produced by stamping them out of metal sheets using huge presses with dies of the appropriate shape. Note that since car shapes are distinctive these dies are unique to a particular model or model range so that the cost of producing them is a highly trans-action-specific investment. Furthermore, car bodies are bulky relative to their value and therefore are costly to transport. The firm will want to minimise transport costs by having the bodies manufactured close to the assembly plant. Thus there will be locational specificity.

The dies themselves are expensive to produce: holding duplicates would raise costs unacceptably. The effect of all this is that the cheapest way of providing the body pressings for the car plant is to have the two sited together and for the two plants to be tied and dependent on each other. Having chosen the site for the assembly plant, the pressings manufacturer will have to engage in highly transaction-specific investment.

The contract between the two firms is unlikely to be able to cover all contingencies because the environment is complex and uncertain and therefore the bounds of rationality will be reached. Since by definition we are *ex post* in a small numbers relation (bilateral monopoly) there is scope for opportunism on both sides. Either party could extort some of the other's profits by threatening to pull out on the grounds of some contingency not covered in the contract.

A straightforward market relationship between two firms

would seem to be out of the question here. What alternatives are there: (a) vertical integration (i.e. the assembly pressings plant is owned and operated as an integrated whole by the assembler); (b) two companies (assembler, pressings manufacturer) set up a joint venture (only makes sense if one party does not have the know-how to operate the other's plant); (c) some sort of arrangement whereby each party makes a bonding payment to the other. This would mean that if one party 'ratted' it would be inflicting a loss on itself, e.g. assembler pays for the dies so that if it pulls out it suffers a loss.

Williamson argues that which form is chosen will depend on the degree of transaction-specific investment and the frequency of the transaction (in terms of our example, frequency relates to the sale of car bodies). This may be shown schematically by Figure 2.2 from Williamson (1979), which is reproduced here as Figure 8.2.

Frequency characteristics	Investment characteristics		
	Non-specific	Mixed	Idiosyncratic
Infrequent	Market	Trilateral	
Frequent	Market governance	Bilateral governance	Unified governance

Figure 8.2

Where a transaction does not involve transaction-specific investment frequency of the transaction does not affect its governance structure and the market is suitable. This is because the non-specificity means that the investment associated with the transaction has alternative uses (or alternative outlets). Thus it is not a small numbers situation: if one party to the contract pulls out a substitute can easily be found; the subject of the transaction in this case is likely to be highly standardised.

In this mode the identity of the parties is not of much relevance and it is really the existence of alternatives in the market that disciplines the parties. The law is only used to settle claims not to deter. Williamson says that this situation corresponds to what McNeil (1978) called classical contract law which sought to emphasise discreteness and presentation. Formal matters were of principal importance.

Where a transaction's frequency is only occasional and investment in it is of a mixed or idiosyncratic character recourse to alternative parties in the event of a contractual breakdown is not so readily possible. The degree of specificity of the investment reduces its alternative uses and in the extremity they are zero. The costs of finding an alternative supplier will also be large. The parties are in a sense locked into the contract.

The parties have an interest in these circumstances in maintaining the contractual relationship. 'Going to law' to resolve a dispute is unlikely to maintain the contractual relationship. In this circumstance both parties will *(ex ante)* have an interest in building into their contract a mechanism for resolving disputes. This will usually involve bringing in a third party to adjudicate or arbitrate such disputes. Thus Williamson refers to the mode of governance here as *trilateral* (it involves three parties). Thus for example, civil engineering contracts usually provide for the resolution of disputes by a consulting engineer or a professional arbitrator. This corresponds to what McNeil has called neoclassical contract-ing – long-term contracts with gaps which are filled at the time they arise with third party assistance.

When a transaction occurs frequently the costs of a transac-tion-specific governance structure become more acceptable – they are spread over many more transactions. Take our problem of supplying car bodies to an assembler. There is a high degree of transaction-specific investment (dies, location) but if there are large numbers of car bodies involved it is likely to be worthwhile for the assembler to undertake the production of pressings himself – vertical integration (unified governance).

With unified governance unforeseen contingencies are not a problem. They can be handled by 'adaptive sequential decision-making'. Even in cases of low frequency transactions it may well be worthwhile integrating if the transaction-specific investment is highly idiosyncratic because then there are no economies of scale to be lost by self-production. Where the transaction-specific investment lies between the non-specific and the idiosyncratic (what Williamson calls mixed) there may be benefits from outside procurement due to limited scale economies and the market nature of the transaction may help to reduce costs. However there is the problem of dealing with contingencies. Both parties have a stake in maintaining the relationship because of the transaction-specific investment and this leads to what Williamson calls 'mutual follow-on agreements'.

Williamson points out that quantity adjustments are likely to be less opportunistic than price adjustments. Price adjustments are zero sum and look like the reallocation of profits. Quantity adjustments (including time) may be seen to be more likely to arise from exogenous events. This is all the more so given that the assets involved are of mixed specificity. Thus it is argued that a bilateral governance structure will evolve which allows routine quantity adjustments.

Williamson identified both unified and bilateral governance with what McNeil calls *relational contracting* in which he described the reference point as not being the original contract but 'the entire relation as it has developed ... [through] time. This may or may not include the "original agreement"; and if it does, may or may not result in great deference being given to it.'

What is the difference between the approach to contract law taken earlier in the chapter and the neo-institutional approach? The former is efficiency-based, therefore it sees the law of contract as providing rules and implicit contract terms which will result in efficient resource allocation. These are designed to discourage inefficient breach and where breach is unavoidable to impose the burden on the party best positioned to bear the cost (best information producer; best risk-bearer). Efficiency is also encouraged by reducing transaction costs and uncertainty (by supplying standard terms). It also provides a framework for regulating abuses that impede or are poorly controlled by market forces. The neo-institutional approach may be seen as superior because it gives greater recognition to the temporal nature of contract and the uncertainty that arises. It sees a crucial role being played by transaction costs. Most of all it sees that contracts involve relations between the parties which differ from those of a sale of goods contract (which might be seen as the paradigm case of the market approach). The neo-institutional approach is also efficiency-oriented but it is more concerned with *procedural* efficiency than *allocative* efficiency.

9 The Efficiency of the Common Law

This book is concerned with how economic analysis can aid our understanding of the law. We have largely – although not exclusively – been concerned with what rules of law might promote efficiency and what are the efficiency characteristics of some existing rules. Implicitly we have been carrying out a *prescriptive* analysis of the law: if you want to promote efficiency these are the rules that you should employ in these specific circumstances. We have, more or less avoided two more fundamental questions: Is the common law efficient? And should the common law be designed to promote efficiency? These questions represent respectively the *positive* economic and the *normative* economic approach to law.

The thrust of much of the literature addressing these questions has come from the work of Richard Posner. It began with his paper 'A Theory of Negligence' published in 1972, and has been further developed in a number of papers by Posner and by Posner and Landes dealing with different areas of the common law. The views of Posner and Landes have not been without their critics. Debates between these groups have been the focus of a number of symposia published in North American legal journals. In this chapter some of the issues in this debate will be rehearsed. One consequence of the debate has been that Posner and his supporters were pushed into addressing the question of why the common law should be efficient. Posner addressed this normatively by arguing that efficiency – by which he means wealth-maximisation – is ethically appealing. We shall spend a little time looking at this. Others responded by looking for a process at work in the courts which would lead to efficient rules surviving and inefficient rules being replaced. This work is associated with Paul Rubin (see Rubin, 1977; 1983). Landes and Posner (1980; 1981a; 1981b) claim that the common law is efficient. What do they mean by this? Do they mean that the law has evolved in such a way that it promotes efficient behaviour? i.e. its *effect* is efficient. This would require an empirical evaluation of specific common law doctrines to see whether they did or did not promote efficiency. It would seem that Posner and Landes are not so much concerned with this notion of the efficiency of the common law as with whether the rules themselves are determined by efficiency considerations. As Tulluck (1980) puts it: 'an efficient legal institution would be one that cannot be changed without making us worse off.'

Frank Michelman (1979) has reformulated the *determinants* version of the efficiency hypothesis thus:

> that the rules, taken as a whole, *tend to look as though they were chosen*, with a view to maximising social wealth (economic output as measured by price) *by judges subscribing to a certain set of ('micro-economic') theoretical principles.*

Notice that this is an 'as if' proposition. It is not that the judges are consciously applying a set of microeconomic principles. They devise a set of legal rules which correspond to those which they would have chosen had they subscribed to a particular set of economic principles. The particular set of economic principles which Posner and Landes argue are involved is the Kaldor–Hicks criterion – or at least a version of the Kaldor–Hicks criterion which only considers wealth not utility.

Posner and his collaborators have examined the law of torts, restitution, contract and privacy and claim that these are all shown to be efficient. The latest application is to the field of products liability (Landes and Posner, 1985).

The efficient common law claim has been criticised on a number of grounds:

(i) *Methodology*. The approach is flawed as positive economics because it does not follow 'proper' scientific method. Patricia Danzon (1985) makes this criticism of

Landes and Posner (1985). The valid way to test a claim such as 'the common law is efficient' is to posit a theory, derive hypotheses from it, and test the resulting predictions. The predictions should be tested on a randomly selected set of doctrines (if not cases). The proper positive scientific method requires the scientist to attempt to refute his theory. This is not what Posner and Landes do: they attempt to *verify* the theory. In practice this is not too different from what most economists do. Mark Blaug (1980) has described the typical approach in the economic literature as 'playing tennis with the net down' as far as refutationist methodology is concerned.

(ii) *Immunising strategies*: Landes and Posner's work may also be criticised on a second ground common to other economists: they invoke immeasurable factors to make apparent anomalies consistent with their predictions. Very often transaction costs or information costs are used to explain an anomaly. This, of course, makes any refutation impossible unless transaction or information costs can actually be measured which is very difficult. This problem is doubly difficult when the theory is being applied to a set of rules rather than actual behaviour. The so-called positive approach can very easily degenerate into rationalisation of existing rules using the theory supposedly being tested. Such an approach may be valid but its validity cannot be tested in the accepted scientific manner. Indeed, it may be argued that it ceases to be a scientific theory and becomes a metaphysical one; a way of viewing how the world works, based on some underlying premise. The acceptability of the theory then depends on the acceptability of its premises.

(iii) *Contextual nature of efficiency*. The notion of efficiency is not an absolute: it is contextually determined, as Victor Goldberg has argued. Thus a rule can only be judged efficient or otherwise with a knowledge of the costs, etc. involved in a particular application. Furthermore, efficiency (particularly when money, rather than utility, is the *numéraire*) can only be judged given the existing distribution of income and wealth, i.e. change the distribution of income and wealth and you may change the monetary valuations individuals attach to a reallocation of resources. Legal rules determine property rights and therefore influence the distribution of income and wealth. Thus evaluating the 'efficiency' of an existing legal rule has a built in bias in favour of the rule.

(iv) *General vs. specific.* Tullock (1980) has argued that the 'law' may be efficient in an *ex ante* sense, in that a set of rules might seem in general to have the prospect of making most people better off most of the time. He, however, argues that such an argument is not so clearly supportable when individual detailed provisions of the law are examined. He basically argues that the Landes–Prosner research simply does not articulate the evidence that is necessary to judge whether a particular law represents an improvement for society, even using the Kaldor–Hicks criterion.

(v) *Nineteenth century basis.* Some writers have argued that the 'efficiency' claim seems plausible in some areas of the law because the doctrines were formulated in the nineteenth century when social thinking and the common law were influenced by market-oriented economics. Thus it is not surprising that these doctrines can be explained by mimicking the market. It may be more difficult for the efficiency claim to be sustained when modern doctrines are examined. Although given the elastic nature of efficiency and immunising stratagems it would not be surprising if they could be encompassed (see Landes and Posner (1985) on products liability).

(vi) *Causal explanation:* The previous line of criticism leads to the next two which in different ways pose a similar question: Given that the evidence on the efficiency claim is fuzzy (or indeed that the hypothesis is non-refutable) is there a *causal explanation* which could persuade us that it is true? Two types of 'causal' explanation have been sought:

(a) What *justificatory force* lies behind the pursuit of efficiency?

(b) If judges merely behave *as if* they were pursuing efficiency, what is the causal explanation for their doing so?

Turning to the first: Why should judges pursue efficiency? What is the normative basis for the efficiency of the common law? Essentially this boils down to the question of what the ethical basis of efficiency is. In part, these criticisms are criticisms of the use of economic analysis in the study of the law but I would argue that economic analysis does not encompass efficiency only but also other considerations such as distribution or the relative deservingness of the different members of society. In conventional economic analysis this wider perspective is articulated via the concept of the *Social Welfare Function*. (See for example, Boadway and Bruce, 1984.)

Posner, however, ploughs a narrow furrow. He argues that not only do the courts pursue efficiency in a Kaldor–Hicks sense but wealth-maximisation is the only justifiable ethical norm. His arguments are set out in *The Economics of Justice*. Posner begins by distinguishing between wealth- maximisation and utilitarianism. He associates the Pareto criterion with utilitarianism. Utilitarianism is rejected because of the difficulty of determining whose preferences should count, whether total utility or average utility should be maximised, the difficulty of interpersonal comparisons of utility, and the danger that individuals will be sacrificed in the name of social utility. The switch to wealth-maximisation removes the problem of interpersonal comparisons of utility, and the danger that individuals will be sacrificed in the name of social utility. The switch to wealth-maximisation removes the problem of interpersonal comparisons and consequently removes the need for the Pareto criterion.

Coleman (1982) argues that Posner supports wealth-maximisation because he cannot accept utilitarianism. But utilitarianism may not be the only alternative (see further below). Anyway where it is possible to compare the two, according to Coleman, wealth-maximisation seems inferior: it only counts the preferences of those with money and therefore does not count everyone's preferences equally.

Posner's second line of argument for wealth-maximisation is one of implied consent. This implied consent or *ex ante* compensation turns out to be based on the premise that there are no systematic distributive effects. People willingly participate in market processes because they know that they will benefit by them on some occasions. However, as Veljanovski (1981) contends, the same presumption cannot be implied in non-market settings. Legally imposed decisions which leave someone worse off cannot be justified on grounds of implied consent just because someone else is made better off!

An alternative justification of simulating the market in judicial decisions is presented by Ronald Dworkin (1986, ch. 8) when he examines the economic analysis of the common law in the context of elaborating his theory of law. The brief discussion possible here cannot do justice to arguments presented in a work running to more than 400 pages which is itself the refinement of ideas explored by its author in a number of previous scholarly works. Dworkin argues that judges are engaged in the enterprise of interpreting the law. He explores three theories of the law which might be seen as informing this interpretive exercise. The first sees the law as a set of conventions: the second as a pragmatic choice in individual cases on the basis of some desired goal such as wealth-maximisation; the third views law as integrity, that is as attempting to answer the requirement that a political community acts in a coherent and principled manner towards all its members. Dworkin concludes that the law-as-integrity model is the most satisfactory. Of relevance here is how he explains accident law within the framework of law as integrity.

Dworkin seems to be conceding that the economic interpretation of the law of unintended accidents (see Chapter 6 above) is the best interpretation that can be put on the cases, i.e. that the least-cost avoider principle applies. It would seem that Dworkin is conceding the validity of the positive economic theory of accident liability, at least as modified by Michelman (1979). However, he clearly does not accept the normative theory: that judges *should* decide cases according to the criterion of wealth-maximisation. He argues that the least-cost avoider principle for determining liability for unintended accidents is consistent with an 'egalitarian' interpretation of private responsibility.

A number of conceptions of equality are explored by Dworkin: the libertarian, the welfare-based (of which utilitarianism is one), material equality and equality of resources. He argues that of these the libertarian and resource-based conceptions of equality are the only ones which are not competitive with the private ambitions which individuals might pursue in the use of their property. The other conceptions would inevitably require repeated redistributions as changes in tastes and technology moved resources away from the distributions which society had designated as desirable. In these cases private decisions are not necessarily harmonised with the social objectives encapsulated within each particular egalitarian conception. Principles based on welfare or material equality could only be obtained within a legal framework which required people to behave in their decision-making in a way which did not disturb the existing distribution of wealth or welfare.

Both the libertarian and the equality of resources conceptions of equality are compatible with private ambitions. The libertarian conception accords people 'natural rights' over property which is recognised by the law as theirs. Thus individuals pursuing their own self-interest in the use of their property are behaving in a manner compatible with the egalitarian principle. The equality of resources approach is based on the notion that governments should secure an equal share of resources for members of society but individuals are left to decide for themselves what the best use of these resources should be. Thus here too, individual decision-making cannot be in conflict with public purpose.

Professor Dworkin then assumes that the equality of resources view fits legal practice no worse than the libertarian view and is better in abstract moral theory. He goes on to argue that in circumstances where the parties are in conflict over the use of their property and they do not have a continuing social relation, the equality of resources principle would require that the least-cost avoider principle should apply. This arises because the equality of resources view requires the parties in a dispute to behave as if the disputed rights had not yet been allocated. In these circumstances the rights would be distributed in the way which equality of resources commends because this minimises the inequality of the achieved distribution. This guide to behaviour would not apply where one of the parties was obviously less well endowed with resources than the other (e.g. is handicapped). Nor would it apply where the parties had a realistic opportunity to work out a compromise through negotiation. If the parties were truly neighbours the particular conflict would be embedded in a more continuous relationship within which the parties might be expected to exercise a degree of 'give and take'. In the absence of such exceptional circumstances it is a practical proposition for each party to assume that the other party is an 'average' person and therefore to behave according to an 'objective' standard such as the reasonable man of ordinary prudence.

It should be noted that these strictures do not apply to legislatures. Dworkin argues that the framers of statutes have a wider remit than individual citizens: to improve the distribution its law has created. Individuals should accept the distribution as created and act as though it were equal. The economic principle is applicable to private behaviour but not to legislation. This excursion into Dworkin's theory of law has been necessarily brief. It has been undertaken not to convince the reader that it is the 'right' theory of law but to show that the broad empirical phenomena cited by Posner are compatible with a widely different moral justification from that which Posner presents.

The second line of argument developed to explain why the common law (or at least many common law doctrines) are efficient is that developed by Rubin (1977; 1983). He argues that it is the process of selection of cases for litigation which results in the efficiency. Rubin's is an *evolutionary* theory of the common law's efficiency. Essentially his theory is about the incentives which different parties have to litigate. Some parties will have a long-run interest in precedent because they are likely to be involved in large numbers of disputes over time. If the existing law is efficient those with a long-run interest do not benefit from challenging it whereas if it is inefficient they do. Thus inefficient laws will be litigated until they are overturned.

Let us now turn to a detailed exposition of Rubin's theory. We shall use, as Rubin does, accident liability. There are two parties, A and B, where A is the defendant and B is the plaintiff. If the existing law places liability on A, this encourages A to spend S_A on accident avoidance and allow N_A accidents to occur. The present value of A's costs are;

$$T_A = S_A + N_A X$$

where X is the accident cost.

If liability were placed on B his costs would be:

$$T_B = S_B + N_B X$$

An efficient law will place liability on the party whose costs are lowest. Thus if $T_B < T_A$, B should be liable.

Who actually bears the costs will depend on the existing case law, for parties such as A and B will be influenced by the precedents governing courts' decisions when they are making decisions about accident avoidance and protection. It is assumed by Rubin that joint action by the parties is not possible. However, although the parties will know the precedents, how the judges would decide an actual case is not known with certainty. If R is the probability that B will win an action then if $R > 0.5$ precedent favours B if $R < 0.5$ precedent favours A. Rubin assumes that judges are likely but not certain to favour precedent.

If the existing case law were not efficient and transaction costs were zero then the parties could bargain around the law. If $T_A > T_B$ but the law favoured B there would be an incentive for A to bribe B to take the precautions. However, it is possible that transaction costs may be greater than $(T_A - T_B)$ and therefore A accepts liability.

A crucial feature of Rubin's analysis is the interest which the parties have in precedent. Some parties will have no interest in precedent since they will be involved in only one such case. This is likely to be the case for individuals. Corporate bodies may well have an ongoing interest in precedent since they may be continuously involved in activities affected by the ruling precedent, e.g. firms, trade unions, governmental bodies and insurance companies. They will not only be involved in particular cases as parties but they will be interested in how the law shapes their ongoing activities. Rubin looks at the situation where both parties are interested in precedent, where only one party is and where neither party is. He argues that where both parties have an ongoing interest in precedent then precedents will evolve towards efficiency. If existing precedents favour the party whose costs are higher then they favour efficiency and there will be no incentive for the party not favoured by precedent to try to overturn these precedents. A party will have an interest in precedent if it is concerned not only with the cost, X, of a given accident but a whole future stream of accident costs, T.

Let us consider an inefficient rule which favours B. An accident occurs and the parties have to decide whether to go to court. If B wins he gets the accident costs X. If A wins he saves X on this accident and T_A in future costs whilst B must start to incur T_B future avoidance costs. Let the court costs for each party be C.

The position of each party is as outlined in Table 9.1 (i). The *net* benefit of going to court for each party is the expected value of going to court less the net outcome by precedent. The expected value of going to court for each party is the outcome if A wins times the probability of A winning plus the outcome if B wins times his probability of winning less the cost of going to court.

The party will be willing to go to court if the net benefit of doing so is positive. If precedent favours B but is inefficient the position is as shown in Table 9.1(i). Here A will go to court if $(1 - R)(X + T_A) > C$ but B will have no desire to go to court since precedent favours him. B thus has an incentive to try to settle out of court since that would leave the precedent undisturbed. An out of court settlement can only be attained if B's expected cost of going to court is greater than A's expected gain. This implies that B can compensate A such that the latter is as well off as he would be if he went to court and B is better off. This requirement for settlement turns out to be that the costs of the parties going to court is greater than the expected gain from A winning, i.e.

$$2C > (1 - R)(T_A - T_B)$$

Rubin refers to $(T_A - T_B)$ as the cost of an inefficient legal rule. We can see that the larger $(T_A - T_B)$ is the greater the incentive to litigate is likely to be, *ceteris paribus*. Similarly, the lower is

Table 9.1
Both Parties Have Long-Run Interest in Precedent
(i) Precedent favours B but is inefficient

	A's position	B's position
Initial position	O	$-X-T_B$
Position by precedent	$-X-T_A$	$+X+T_B$
Net outcome by precedent	$-X-T_A$	O
Cost of going to court	$-C$	$-C$
(a) Court finds for A	O	$-X-T_B$
(B) Court finds for B	$-X-T_A$	O
Expected value of going to court $[(1-R)(a)+R(b)-C]$	$-R(X+T_A)-C$	$-(1-R)(X+T_B)-C$
Net benefit of going to court	$-R(X+T_A)-C-(-X-T_A)$ $= (1-R)(X+T_A)-C$	$-(1-R)(X+T_B)-C$ $=-[(1-R)(X+T_B)+C]$
Litigate?	*Yes if* $(1-R)(X+T_A)>C$	No
Requirement for settlement	$(1-R)(X+T_B)+C>(1-R)(X+T_A)-C$ *i.e.* $2C>(1-R)(T_A-T_B)$	
Outcome	If (T_A-T_B) is large enough given C and R, A will go to court.	
Effect on law	A will litigate till law changed.	

R (the probability of the court finding for B) the greater the incentive to litigate. Conversely, the more entrenched the precedents (i.e. the higher R) the less incentive there is to litigate. The lower are court costs then the greater incentive there is to litigate.

If the current rule is efficient $T_B > T_A$, and there is no incentive to litigate.

If the variables are such that there is an incentive to litigate the court is likely to find in favour of B (since $R > 0.5$) and the inefficient rule stays in force. However, according to Rubin, A still has an incentive to litigate when $(I - R)(T_A - T_B) > 2C$ on each occasion when an accident occurs until a court finds in A's favour. Then the law has become efficient. But B will never have an incentive to try to overturn the new rule. Thus anyone looking at this new situation would observe that it was effi-

Table 9.1 (continued)

(ii)   Precedent favours A and is efficient

	A's position	B's position
Initial position	O	$-X-T_B$
Position by precedent	O	O
Net outcome by precedent	O	$-X-T_B$
Cost of going to court	$-C$	$-C$
(a) Court finds for A	O	$-X-T_B$
(b) Court finds for B	$-X-T_A$	O
Expected value of going to court $[(1-R)(a) + R(b) -C]$	$-R(X+T_A) - C$	$-(1-R)(X+T_B) - C$
Net benefit of going to court	$-R(X+T_A) - C$ $= [R(X+T_A) + C]$	$-(1-R)(X+T_B) - C$ $-[-(X+T_B)]$ $= R(X+T_B) - C$
Litigate?	No	Yes if $R(X+T_B) > C$
Requirement for settlement	$R(X+T_A) + C > R(X+T_B) - C$ $2C > R(T_B-T_A)$	
Outcome	Since the precedent favouring A is efficient by assumption $T_A > T_B$ ∴ requirements for settlement always holds.	
Effect on law	The law will continue to favour A	

cient: not because the judges pursue efficiency but because of the process by which the law evolves. Part (ii) of Table 9.1 illustrates the case where the precedent favours A and is efficient. Here the situation favours settlement.

Notice that it is the fact that both parties have a long-run interest in precedent that generates the efficient result. If only one party has such an interest the law will evolve to favour him whether that would be efficient or not. This is illustrated in Table 9.2(i) in which it is assumed that the current precedent favours A but he does not have a long-run interest in precedent while B does. Thus A is only interest in X, the cost of the accident, while B is interested in future avoidance costs and accident costs. Thus A will not wish to go to court since the net

Table 9.2
Only One Party Has Long-Run Interest in Precedent
(i) B has long-run interest in precedent but precedent favours A

	A's position	B's position
Initial position	O	$-X-T_B$
Position by precedent	O	O
Net outcome by precedent	O	$-(X + X_B)$
Cost of going to court	$-C$	$-C$
(a) Court finds for A	O	$-(X + T_B)$
(b) Court finds for B	$-X$	O
Expected value of going to court $[(1-R)(a) + R(B) - C]$	$-RX-C$	$-(1-R)(X+T_B) - C$
Net benefit of going to court	$-RX-C$ $=-[RX + C]$	$-(1-R)(X+T_B)$ $-C+(X+T_B)$ $= R(X+T_B) - C$
Litigate?	No	Yes if $R(X+T_B) > C$
Requirement for settlement	$RX + C > R(X + T_B) - C$ i.e. $2C > R(T_B)$	
Outcome	If $R(T_B) > 2C$, B will go to court	
Effect on law	B will continue to litigate until law is changed	

benefit to him of doing so is $R(-X) - C$ which is negative. B *may* wish to go to court because his net benefit of court action is:

$$R(X) + R(T_B) - C$$

Therefore A will be willing to yield $(-R(X) - C)$ to avoid court action and B stands to get $R(X) + R(T_B) - C$ from court action. Litigation will take place if:

$$R(X) + R(T_B) - C > R(X) + C$$

i.e. $R(T_B) > 2C$. Thus unless R is small (i.e. precedent strongly favours A, or court costs are high) it will be worth B's while to go to court to try to change the law and he will have this

Table 9.2 *(continued)*

(ii) *B has long-run interest in precedent and precedent favours B*

	A's position	B's position
Initial position	O	$-X-T_B$
Position by precedent	$-X$	$X+T_B$
Net outcome by precedent	$-X$	O
Cost of going to court	$-C$	$-C$
(a) Court finds for A	O	$-(X+T_B)$
(b) Court finds for B	$-X$	O
Expected value of going to court $[(1-R)(a) + R(b) - C]$	$-RX-C$	$-(1-R)(X+T_B) - C$
Net benefit of going	$-[RX + C] + X$ $= (1 - R)X - C$	$-[(1-R)(X+T_B) + C]$
Litigate?	Yes if $(1-R)X > C$	No
Requirement for settlement	$(1-R)(X+T_B) - C > (1 - R)X - C$ i.e. $2C > -(1 -R)T_B$	
Outcome	Requirement for out of court settlement always holds	
Effect on law	The law will continue to favour B	

incentive every time he is involved in an accident. At some point a judge may rule in B's favour and the law will change. The next time an accident occurs involving B part (ii) of Table 9.2 is relevant. B has no incentive to go to court to change the law although the new A does if

$$(1 - R)X > C$$

B has no incentive to go to court since the net benefit of doing so is negative. In this situation B always stands to lose more from going to court than A stands to gain. Therefore the situation always favours an out of court settlement. Thus the precedent favouring B will remain undisturbed.

Notice this result holds whether the law is efficient or not. Thus where only one party has a long-run interest in precedent the law will favour that party. Rubin argues that nuisance law's evolution in the nineteenth century might be seen in that light: factory-owners had a long-run interest in precedent whereas property-owners did not. Therefore the law evolved in favour the externality-creating factories.

If neither party has a long-run interest in precedent Rubin argues that cases will not be litigated and existing law will remain unchanged. This is illustrated in Table 9.3. The net benefit of going to court for A is $[(1 - R)X - C]$ and the cost of going to court for B is $[C + (1 - R)X]$. Therefore B will be willing to settle out of court for at least as much as A can get by going to court.

It should be recognised that Rubin's analysis assumes that A and B agree on the value of R. Clearly if A and B differ in their judgement as to who will win the likelihood of litigation is increased.

Table 9.3
Neither Party Has Long-Run Interest in Precedent
Precedent Favours B

	A's position	B's position
Initial position	O	$-X$
Position by precedent	$-X$	$+X$
Net outcome of precedent	$-X$	O
Cost of going to court	$-C$	$-C$
(a) If court finds for A	O	$-X$
(b) If court finds for B	$-X$	O
Expected value of going to court $[(1 - R)(a) + R(b) - C]$	$-RX-C$	$(1-R)(-X) - C$
Net benefit of going to court	$-RX-C- (-X)$ $= (1-R)X-C$	$(1-R)(-X) - C$ $= -[C+(1-R)X]$
Litigate?	Yes if $(1-R)X > C$	No
Requirement for settlement	$C + (1-R)X > (1-R)X - C$	
Outcome	Settle out of court	
Effect on law	None	

This chapter has examined the positive and normative theories of the efficiency of the common law. It has been argued that on methodological grounds the descriptive claim of Landes and Posner cannot be accepted. The normative claim has been seen to lack justificatory force. On the other hand, Rubin's evolutionary theory of the common law does provide a mechanism by which the efficiency of certain doctrines (which involve parties with a continuing interest) could emerge. However, this is not a general theory. It depends on the nature of the parties affected by the specific doctrines. Once again we see that detailed analysis undermines claims for 'general laws' which is only to be expected by an economic realist.

References

Ackerman, B. A., *Economic Foundation of Property Law* (Boston: Little Brown, 1975).

Agnello, R. J. & Donnelley, L. P., 'Price and Property Rights in the Fisheries', *Southern Economic Journal*, 4 (1975) pp. 253–62.

Attiyah, P. S., *An Introduction to the Law of Contract* (Oxford, Clarendon Press, 3rd edn 1981a).

Attiyah, P. S., 'The Theoretical Basis of Contract Law – An English Perspective', *International Review of Law and Economics*, 1(2) (1981b), pp. 183–205.

Baker, C. E., 'The Ideology of the Economic Analysis of Law', *Philosophy and Public Affairs*, 5(1) (1975), pp. 3–38.

Barton, J. H., 'The Economic Basis of Damages for Breach of Contract', *Journal of Legal Studies*, 1(2) (1972), pp. 277–304.

Becker, G. & Landes, W. M. (eds), *Essays in the Economics of Crime and Punishment* (1974).

Bell, F. W., 'Technological Externalities and Common Property Resources: A Study of the US Northern Lobster Fishery', *Journal of Political Economy*, 83 (1975).

Blaug, M., *The Methodology of Economics*, (Cambridge: Cambridge University Press, 1980).

Boadway, R. W. & Bruce, N., *Welfare Economics* (Oxford: Basil Blackwell, 1984).

Bottomley, A., 'The Effect of Common Ownership of Land upon Resource Allocation in Tripolitania', *Land Economics* (1963).

Brown, J. P., 'Toward an Economic Theory of Liability', *Journal of Legal Studies*, 2(2) (1973), pp. 323–49.

Bucknall, B. D., 'In Search of the Equitable Levy: New Approaches to the Imposition of Condition upon Development in Ontario', *Municipal and Planning Law Report*, 11 (1981), p. 133.

Burrows, P. & Veljanovski, C. G., (eds), *The Economic Approach to*

Law (London: Butterworths, 1981).

Calabresi, G., *The Cost of Accidents: A Legal and Economic Analysis* (New Haven: Yale University Press, 1970).

Calabresi, G. & Melamed, A. D., 'Property Rules, Liability Rules and Inalienability: One View of the Cathedral', *Harvard Law Review*, 85(6) (1972), pp. 1089–128.

Caldwell, B., *Beyond Positive Economics*, (London: Allen & Unwin, 1983).

Call, S. T. & Holahan, W. L., *Microeconomics* (Belmont: Wadsworth, 2nd edn, 1980).

Chamberlin, E. H., *Monopolistic Competition* (Cambridge, Mass.: Harvard University Press, 1933).

Clark, A., 'The Conceptual Basis of Product Liability', *The Modern Law Review*, 50 (1985), pp. 325–39.

Coase, R. H., 'The Nature of the Firm', *Economica*, 5 (1937).

Coase, R. H. 'The Problem of Social Cost', *Journal of Law and Economics*, 3(1) (1960), pp. 1–44.

Coase, R. H., 'Economics and Contiguous Disciplines', in Perlmann, M. (ed.), *The Organisation and Retrieval of Economic Knowledge* (London: Macmillan, 1977).

Coleman, J. M., 'The Normative Basis of Economic Analysis: A Critical Review of Richard Posner's *The Economics of Justice*', *Stanford Law Review*, 34(5) (1982), pp. 1105–31.

Cooter, R., 'The Cost of Coase', *Journal of Legal Studies*, 22 (1982), pp. 1–34.

Danzon, P. M. 'Comments on Landes and Posner: A Positive Economic Analysis of Products Liability', *Journal of Legal Studies*, 14(3) (1985), pp. 569–74.

Davies, K., *The Law of Compulsory Purchase and Compensation* (London: Butterworths, 4th edn 1984).

De Alessi, L., 'The Economics of Property Rights: A Review of the Evidence', *Research in Law and Economics* (1980).

Deans, M., 'Planning Conditions and the Courts', *Scottish Planning Law and Practice* (1980), p. 10.

Dunlop, B. J., 'Compensation for Personal Injuries', in Evans and Trebilcock, M. J. (eds), *Lawyers and the Public Interest* (Toronto: Butterworths, 1981).

Dworkin, R. M. 'Is Wealth a Value?', *Journal of Legal Studies*, 9(2) (1980) pp. 191–226.

Dworkin, R., *Law's Empire* (London: Fontana, 1986).

Ellickson, R. C., 'Alternatives to Zoning: Covenants, Nuisance Rules and Fines as Land Use Controls', *University of Chicago Law Review*, 40(4) (1973), pp. 681–781.

Ellickson, R. C. and Tarlock, A. D. *Land Use Controls: Cases and Materials* (Boston: Little, Brown, 1981).

Epstein, R. A., 'A Theory of Strict Liability', *Journal of Legal Studies*, 2(1) (1973), pp. 151–221.

Epstein, R. A. 'Unconscionability: A Critical Approach', *Journal of Law and Economics*, 18(2) (1975), pp. 293–315.

Epstein, R. A., 'Nuisance Law: Corrective Justice and its Utilitarian Constraints', *Journal of Legal Studies*, 8(1) (1979) pp. 49–102.

Epstein, R. A., *Modern Products Liability Law* (Westport, Conn.: Quorum Books, 1980).

Farrier, D. and McAuslin, P., 'Compensation, Participation and the Compulsory Acquisition of Homes' in Garner (1975).

Fischel, W. A. *The Economics of Zoning Laws* (Baltimore and London: The Johns Hopkins University Press, 1985).

Fleming, J. G., *An Introduction to the Law of Torts* (Oxford: Clarendon Press, 1968).

Fleming, J. G. *The Law of Torts* (London: The Law Book Company, 5th edn, 1976).

Freilich, R. H. and Dierker, R., 'Eminent Domain in American Jurisprudence', in Garner (1975).

Friedman, L. A., *A History of American Law* (New York: Simon and Schuster, 1973).

Furubotn, E. and Pejovich, S., 'Property Rights and Economic Theory: A Survey of Recent Literature', *Journal of Economic Literature*, X(4) (1972), pp. 1137–63.

Garner, J. F., *Compensation for Compulsory Purchase: A Comparative Study* (London: UK Committee for Comparative Law, 1975).

Gerner, J. L. and Bryant, W. K. 'The Price of a Warranty: The Case of Refrigerators', *Journal of Consumer Affairs*, 12 (1978), pp. 30–47.

Gerner, J. L. and Bryant, W. K., 'Appliance Warranties as a Market Signal', *Journal of Consumer Affairs*, 15 (1981), pp. 75–86.

Goetz, C. J. and Scott, R. E., 'Enforcing Promises: An Examination of the Basis of Contract', *Yale Law Journal*, 89 (1980), p. 1261.

Goldberg, V. P., 'The Economics of Product Safety and Imperfect Information', *Bell Journal of Economics*, 5(2) (1974), pp. 683–88.

Goldberg, V. P., 'Relational Exchange and Complex Contracts', *American Behavioural Scientist*, 23(3) (1980), pp. 337–52.

Goldberg, V. P., 'A Relational Exchange Perspective on the Employment Relationship', in Stephen, F. H. (ed.), *Firms, Organization and Labour* (London: The Macmillan Press, 1984).

Grant, M., *Urban Planning Law* (London: Sweet & Maxwell, 1982).

Haddock, D. & Curran, C., 'An Economic Theory of Comparative Negligence', *Journal of Legal Studies*, 14 (1985), pp. 49–72.

Hansmann, H., 'The Current State of Law and Economics Scholarship', *Journal of Legal Education*, 33(2) (1983), pp. 217–36.

Harris, D., 'Accident Compensation in New Zealand', *Modern Law Review*, 37 (1972), p. 361.

Harris, D., Ogus, A. I. & Phillips, J., 'Contract Remedies and the Consumer Surplus', *Law Quarterly Review*, 95 (1979), pp. 581–610.

Harrison, G. and McKee, M., 'Experimental Evaluation of the Coase Theorem', *Journal of Law and Economics*, 25 (1985), pp. 653–70.

Hayek, F. A., 'The Use of Knowledge in Society', *American Economic Review*, 35(4) (1945), pp. 519–30.

Heineke, J. M. (ed.) *Economic Models of Criminal Behaviour* (Amsterdam: North Holland, 1978).

Henderson, A. M., 'Consumers' Surplus and the Compensating Variation', *Review of Economic Studies*, 8 (1941), p. 117.

Hicks, J. 'The Four Consumers' Surpluses', *Review of Economic Studies*, 11 (1943), p. 31.

HMSO, *Planning Gain*, Report by the Property Advisory Group (1981).

Hoffman, E. & Spitzer, M., 'The Coase Theorem – Some Empirical Tests', *Journal of Law and Economics*, 25(1) (1982), pp. 73–98.

Horwitz, M. J., *The Transformation of American Law, 1790–1860* (Cambridge, Mass: Havard University Press, 1977).

Hudec, A. T., 'Municipal Exactions and the Subdivision Approval Process: A Legal and Economic Analysis', *University of Toronto Faculty of Law Review*, 38 (1980), 106.

Kennedy, D., 'Cost-Benefit Analysis of Entitlement Problems: A Critique', *Stanford Law Review*, 33(3) (1981), pp. 387–445.

Klevorick, A. K., 'Reflections on The Current State of Law-and-Economics Scholarship', *Journal of Legal Education*, 33(2) (1985), pp. 237–46.

Knetsch, J. L., *Property Rights and Compensation – Compulsory Acquisition and Other Losses* (Toronto: Butterworths, 1983).

Knetsch, J. L. & Sinden, J. A., 'Willingness to Pay and Compensation Demanded: Experimental Evidence of an Unexpected Disparity in Measures of Value', *Quarterly Journal of Economics*, 99 (1984), p. 507.

Kornhauser, L. A., 'A Guide to the Perplexed Claims of Efficiency in the Law', *Hofstra Law Review*, 8(3) (1980), pp. 591–639.

Kronman, A. T., 'Specific Performance', *University of Chicago Law*

Review, 45(2) (1978), pp. 351–82.

Kronman, A. T. & Posner, R. A. (eds), *The Economics of Contract Law* (Boston: Little, Brown, 1979).

Landes, W. & Posner, R. A., 'Joint and Multiple Torts: An Economic Analysis', *Journal of Legal Studies*, 9(3) (1980), pp. 517–56.

Landes, W. & Posner, R. A., 'The Positive Economic Theory of Tort Law', *Georgia Law Review*, 15(4) (1981a), pp. 851–924.

Landes, W. & Posner, R. A., 'An Economic Theory of Intentional Torts', *International Review of Law and Economics*, 2(1) (1981b), pp. 127–54.

Landes, W. M. & Posner, R. A., 'A Positive Economic Analysis of Products Liability', *Journal of Legal Studies*, 14(3) (1985), pp. 535–68.

Libecap, G., 'Economic Variables and the Development of the Law: The Case of Western Mineral Rights', *Journal of Economic History*, 38(2) (1978), pp. 338–62.

Libecap, G., 'Government Support of Private Claims to Public Minerals: Western Mineral Rights', *Business History Review*, 43 (1979).

Libecap, G. & Wiggins, S., 'The Influence of Contractual Failure on Regulation: The Case of Oilfield Unitization', *Journal of Political Economy*, 93(4) (1985), pp. 690–714.

Loughlin, M., 'Planning Gain: Law, Policy and Practice', *Oxford Journal of Legal Studies*, 1 (1981), p. 61.

Machlup, E., 'Positive and Normative Economics: an Analysis of the Ideas', in Heilbroner, R. L. (ed.), *Economic Means and Social Ends* (Englewood Cliffs, N.J.: Prentice Hall, 1969).

MacNeil, I. R., 'Contracts: Adjustment of Long-Term Economic Relations Under Classical Neoclassical and Relational Contract Law', *Northwestern University Law Review*, 72(6) (1978), pp. 854–965.

MacNeil, I. R., 'Economic Analysis of Contractual Relations', in Burrows & Veljanovski (1981).

Makuch, S., *Canadian Municipal and Planning Law* (Toronto: Carswell Co., 1983).

McKean, R. N., 'Products Liability: Implications of Some Changing Property Rights', *Quarterly Journal of Economics*, 84(4) (1970), pp. 611–26.

McLachlan, H. V. & Swales, J. K., 'Friedman's Methodology: A Comment on Botland', *Journal of Economic Studies*, 9(1) (1982), pp. 19–34.

Michelman, F. I., 'Property, Utility and Fairness: Comments on the Ethical Foundations of "Just Compensation"' *Harvard Law*

Review, 80(b) (1967), pp. 1165–258.

Michelman, F. I., 'Pollution as a Tort: A Non-accidental Perspective on Calabresi's Costs', *Yale Law Journal*, 80(5) (1971), pp. 647–86.

Michelman, F. I., 'A Comment on Some Uses and Abuses of Economics in Law', *University of Chicago Law Review*, 46(2) (1979), pp. 307–15.

Mishan, E. J., 'Pareto Optimality and the Law', *Oxford Economic Papers*, 19 (3) (1967), pp. 247–87.

Montgomery, J. E. and Owen D. G., 'Reflections on the Theory and Administration of Strict Tort Liability for Defective Products', *South Carolina Law Review*, 27 (1976), p. 803.

Ogus, A. I. & Richardson, G., 'Economics and the Environment: A Study of Private Nuisance', *Cambridge Law Journal*, 36(2) (1977), pp. 284–325.

Ogus, A. I. & Veljanovski, C. G. (eds), *Readings in the Economics of Law and Regulation* (Oxford: Oxford University Press, 1984).

Oi, W. Y., 'The Economics of Product Safety', *Bell Journal of Economics*, 4(1) (1973), pp. 3–28.

Pauly, M., 'The Economics of Moral Hazard', *American Economic Review*, 58 (1968), pp. 531–7.

Pelzman, S., 'The Effects of Automobile Safety Regulations', *Journal of Political Economy*, 86 (1978), pp. 677–723.

Polinsky, A. M., 'Controlling Externalities and Protecting Entitlements: Property Right Liability Rule and Tax-Subsidy Approaches', *Journal of Legal Studies*, 8(1) (1979), pp. 1–49.

Polinsky, A. M., 'On the Choice between Property Rules and Liability Rules', *Economic Inquiry*, 18(2) (1980a), pp. 233–46.

Polinsky, A. M. 'Resolving Nuisance Disputes: The Simple Economics of Injunctive and Damage Remedies', *Stanford Law Review*, 32(b) (1980b), 1075–112.

Posner, R. A., *Economic Analysis of Law* (Boston: Little, Brown, 1st edn 1972a, 2nd edn 1977).

Posner, R. A., 'A Theory of Negligence', *Journal of Legal Studies*, 1(1) (1972b), pp. 29–96.

Posner, R. A., 'The Economic Approach to Law', *Texas Law Review*, 53(7) (1975), pp. 757–82.

Posner, R. A., 'Some Uses and Abuses of Economics in Law', *University of Chicago Law Review*, 46(2) (1979), pp. 281–306.

Posner, R. A. *Tort Law – Cases and Economic Analysis* (Boston: Little, Brown, 1982).

Priest, G. L., 'A Theory of the Consumer Warranty', *Yale Law Journal*, 90(6) (1981), pp. 1297–352.

Priest, G. L. & Klein, B., 'The Selection of Dispute for Litigation',

Journal of Legal Studies, 23(1) (1984), pp. 1–56.

Regan, D. H., 'The Problem of Social Cost Revisited', *Journal of Law and Economics*, 15(2) (1972), pp. 427–37.

Rowan-Robinson, J. & Young, E. *Planning by Agreement in Scotland: The Law and Practice* (Scottish Planning Law and Practice, 1982).

Rubin, P. H., 'Why is the Common Law Efficient', *Journal of Legal Studies*, 6(1) (1977), pp. 51–64.

Rubin, P. H., *Business Firms and the Common Law: The Evolution of Efficient Rules* (New York: Praeger, 1983).

Schoemaker, P. J. H. 'The Expected Utility Model: Its Variants, Purposes, Evidence and Limitations', *Journal of Economic Literature*, 20 (1982), pp. 529–63.

Schwartz, A., 'The Case for Specific Performance', *Yale Law Journal*, 89 (1979), p. 271.

Shackle, G. L. S. *Expectation in Economics* (Cambridge: Cambridge University Press, 2nd edn 1952).

Shackle, G. L. S., *Decision, Order and Time in Human Affairs* (Cambridge: Cambridge University Press, 2nd edn 1969).

Shackle, G. L. S., *Expectation, Enterprise and Profit* (London: George Allen and Unwin, 1970).

Shavel, S., 'Damage Measures for Breach of Contract', *Bell Journal of Economics*, 11(2) (1980), pp. 466–90.

Siegan, B. H., *Land Use without Zoning* (Lexington, Mass.: Health-Lexington Books, 1972).

Slawson, W. D., 'Standard Form Contracts and the Democratic Control of Lawmaking Power, *Harvard Law Review*, 84(1), 1971, pp. 529–66.

Stephen, F. H., *The Economic Analysis of Producers' Cooperatives* (London: Macmillan, 1984).

Stephen, F. H., 'Property rules and liability rules in the regulation of land development: An analysis of development control in Great Britain and Ontario', *International Review of Law and Economics* (forthcoming 1987).

Stephen, F. H. & Young, E., 'An Economic Insight on the Judicial Control of Planning Authorities' Discretion', *Urban Law and Policy*, (1985).

Stigler, G. J., 'The Economics of Information', *Journal of Political Economy*, 69 (1961), pp. 213–25.

Trebilcock, M. J., 'The Doctrine of Inequality of Bargaining Power: Post Benthamite Economics in the House of Lords', *University of Toronto Law Journal*, 26(4) (1976), pp. 359–85.

Trebilcock, M. J., 'An Economic Approach to the Doctrine of

Unconscionability' in Reiter, B. J. & Swan, J. (eds), *Studies in Contract Law* (Toronto: Butterworths, 1980).

Trebilcock, M. J., 'The Prospects of "Law and Economics": A Canadian Perspective', *Journal of Legal Education*, 33(2) (1983), pp. 288–93.

Trebilcock, M. J. & Dewees, D., 'Judicial Control of Standard Form Contracts', in Burrows and Veljanovski (1981).

Tromans, S., 'Nuisance – Prevention or Payment?', *Cambridge Law Journal*, 41(1) (1982), pp. 87–109.

Tullock, G., 'Two Kinds of Efficiency', *Hofstra Law Review*, 8(5) (1980), pp. 659–69.

Turvey, R., 'On the Divergence between Social Cost and Private Cost', *Economica*, 30 (1963), pp. 309–13.

Underwood, J. *Development Control: A Review of Research and Current Issues* (Progress in Planning, 1981).

Veljanovski, C. G., 'The Economic Theory of Tort Liability – Toward a Corrective Justice Approach', in Burrows and Veljanovski (eds) (1981).

Veljanovski, C. G., 'Wealth Maximization Law and Ethics – On the Limits of Economic Efficiency', *International Review of Law and Economics*, 1(1) (1981b), pp. 5–28.

Veljanovski, C. G., *The New Law-and-Economics – A Research Review* (Oxford: Centre for Socio-Legal Studies, 1982a).

Veljanovski, C. G., 'The Coase Theorems and The Economic Theory of Markets and Law', *Kyklos*, 35(1) (1982b), pp. 66–81.

Waterson, M., *Economic Theory of the Industry* (Cambridge: Cambridge University Press, 1984).

Widdicombe, D. & Moore, V., 'A General Survey of English Law', in Garner (1975).

Wiggins, S., & Libecap, G., 'Oil Field Unitization Contractual Failure in the Presence of Imperfect Information', *American Economic Review*, 75 (1985).

Williamson, O. E., *Markets and Hierarchies: Analysis and Anti-Trust Implications* (New York: Free Press, 1975).

Williamson, O. E., 'Transaction Cost Economics: The Governance of Contractual Relations', *Journal of Law and Economics*, 22(2) (1979), pp. 233–61.

Williamson, O. E., *The Economic Institutions of Capitalism* (New York: Free Press, 1985).

Wolpin, K. I., 'An Economic Analysis of Crime and Punishment in England and Wales, 1894–1969', *Journal of Political Economy*, 86 (1978).

Young, E. & Rowan-Robinson, J., *Scottish Planning Law and Procedure* (Glasgow: Wm Hodge, 1986).

Index